THE BANK DIRECTOR'S VALUATION HANDBOOK

What Every Director Must Know About Valuation

THE BANK DIRECTOR'S VALUATION HANDBOOK

What Every Director Must Know About Valuation

MERCER CAPITAL

THE BANK DIRECTOR'S VALUATION HANDBOOK

What Every Director Must Know About Valuation

ISBN: 978-0-9700698-6-3

Peabody Publishing LP
5860 Ridgeway Center Parkway, Suite 400
Memphis, Tennessee 38120
Tel: 800.769.0967
Fax: 901.685.2199

PREFACE

WHY IS THIS HANDBOOK IMPORTANT?

Valuation issues intersect with a bank's affairs more often than you may imagine, and they are likely to arise during your tenure as a director or manager. These valuation issues might include merger and acquisition activity, an employee stock ownership plan, capital planning, litigation, or financial planning, among others. Mercer Capital has been working with financial institutions for over 25 years and has provided valuation and other financial consulting services to thousands of clients. We find that most of our clients have the same basic questions about these important valuation issues. This handbook is written to address many of these questions and to provide useful information for bank directors and managers when valuation needs emerge. It is unique in that it focuses specifically on valuation-related issues, and is designed to be a ready resource rather than an academic treatise.

WHO SHOULD READ THIS HANDBOOK?

This handbook is written specifically for bank directors and managers. It provides basic information and insight into those circumstances that involve valuation and other financial consulting. Each chapter addresses a valuation issue that might surface at your financial institution. Meant to stand alone, the chapters summarize the key issues on which you should focus and provide insight and a vocabulary to assist you in asking the right questions of your professional advisors.

STRUCTURE OF THE HANDBOOK

This handbook is a ready reference guide to focus your thinking. No one expects you to be an expert in all matters when faced with a valuation issue. Consequently, we group the chapters into broader sections that encompass areas where valuation issues converge most often with your bank's affairs. Hopefully, this will make it easier for you to identify which section covers a particular subject. Additionally, each chapter in the handbook is written to provide a quick primer on the particular subject that it addresses. Section One provides a basic overview of valuation, Sections Two through Six provide common examples of valuation issues you may encounter, and Section Seven contains resource information such as an addendum addressing current issues, a bibliography, and glossary.

» **Section One - Introduction to Valuation.** It is important for bank directors and managers to have at least an elementary understanding of the valuation process and the basic concepts of valuation as they relate to financial institutions. Valuation fundamentals such as the levels of value, the standard of value, valuation approaches, and others are discussed.

» **Section Two - Compensation and Employee Benefit Plans**. Banks often issue stock options to executive officers or create an employee benefit plan. Valuation issues stem from determining the value of the bank's stock for transactions within an employee benefit plan or for stock options in setting the option price, tax compliance related to the options, and the accounting for the options.

» **Section Three - Stock Transactions**. Transactions in a bank's stock may occur in many different contexts. For example, a bank's treasury may purchase shares from shareholders needing liquidity, the bank may sell new shares to raise additional capital, or a shareholder may gift shares to a descendant. Different valuation issues may emerge in each of these situations. Three common matters that may trigger valuation issues are transactions related to estate and gift tax issues, raising capital, and buy-sell agreements.

» **Section Four - Strategic Alternatives**. Management and directors may evaluate specific transactions designed to enhance shareholder value, such as an acquisition, divestiture, or share repurchase. Unless the valuation issues connected with the transaction are understood, management and directors cannot assess the merits of the transaction sufficiently.

» **Section Five - Financial Reporting**. As accounting rules change, more and more assets are carried at fair value on a bank's balance sheet, rather than historical cost. Therefore, the quality of a bank's financial statements depends upon its measurements of fair value, which often requires a valuation.

» **Section Six - Statutory and Legal Concepts.** Occasionally situations develop where litigation is threatened or actually occurs, and managers and directors should be aware of the types of valuation services that could be helpful in these circumstances. Two areas where valuation issues related to litigated matters might arise are transactions that trigger dissenters' rights and the divorce of a shareholder.

» **Section Seven - Conclusion.** Given the number of changes in the banking industry in 2008 and the potential for these changes to affect the banking landscape for years to come, we would be remiss not to address the recent financial crisis and its potential impact on bank valuation issues going forward. Consequently, this section includes two addenda that address two government initiatives resulting from the economic crisis of late 2007 and 2008, the Capital Purchase Program ("CPP") and IRS Notice 2008-83, which is a tax incentive that could be beneficial for banks considering an acquisition. In addition, an extensive bibliography and a glossary are provided. The bibliography contains a number of useful websites, books, and articles. The glossary defines a number of terms that are referenced in the handbook and are commonly used in valuation reports.

CONCLUSION

This handbook was written in mid-to-late 2008. The last twelve months have been an extraordinarily turbulent time in the financial markets, and the situation may not stabilize for some time. Our purpose in noting this is not to place this handbook in a particular time setting, but to remind the reader of the impact of changes in circumstances as time passes. On many occasions, the passage of time matters greatly in activities involving business valuation.

Please note that as of the drafting of this handbook, the Troubled Asset Relief Program continues to evolve, and we will provide appropriate updates to the addendum as conditions warrant via our website at www.mercercapital.com.

ABOUT THE AUTHORS

ANDREW K. GIBBS, CFA, CPA/ABV

Andrew K. Gibbs ("Andy") leads Mercer Capital's Financial Institutions Group. Andy provides valuation and corporate advisory services to financial institutions for purposes including mergers and acquisitions, employee stock ownership plans, profit sharing plans, estate and gift tax planning and compliance matters, as well as corporate planning and reorganizations. In addition, he actively participates in projects involving compliance with SFAS 141R and 142, which entail, for example, the identification and valuation of intangible assets under SFAS 141R and impairment testing under SFAS 142. Andy is a CFA charterholder from the CFA Institute. In addition, he holds the Accredited in Business Valuation designation from the AICPA and is a certified public accountant.

JAMES D. WILSON, JR.

James D. Wilson, Jr. ("Jay") is a senior member of Mercer Capital's Financial Institutions Group. He is involved in the valuation of financial institutions as well as operating entities in the retail, services, and manufacturing industries. Circumstances giving rise to the engagements Jay is involved with include corporate planning and reorganizations, litigation support, employee stock ownership plans, transaction advisory, fairness opinions, and estate and gift tax planning and compliance matters. In addition, he actively participates in projects involving compliance with SFAS 141R and 142.

Contributing Authors

KENNETH W. PATTON, ASA

Kenneth W. Patton ("Ken") serves as president of Mercer Capital, and is a senior member of Mercer Capital's Financial Institutions Group. Ken has over 35 years of experience working with financial institutions. Prior to joining Mercer Capital, Ken worked in the banking industry, first as a national bank examiner and then at Union Planters National Bank in Memphis. Ken holds the Accredited Senior Appraiser designation from the American Society of Appraisers.

LAURA J. HOFFMEISTER

Laura J. Hoffmeister is a member of Mercer Capital's Financial Institutions Group. Circumstances giving rise to the engagements Laura is involved with include goodwill impairment testing, corporate planning and reorganizations, employee stock ownership plans, and estate and gift tax planning and compliance matters.

KRISTIN C. BECKMAN

Kristin C. Beckman is a member of Mercer Capital's Financial Institutions Group. Circumstances giving rise to the engagements Kristin is involved with include goodwill impairment testing, corporate planning and reorganizations, employee stock ownership plans, and estate and gift tax planning and compliance matters.

MADELEINE C. GILMAN

Madeleine C. Gilman ("Maddie") is a member of Mercer Capital's Financial Institutions Group. Circumstances giving rise to the engagements Maddie is involved with include goodwill impairment testing, corporate planning and reorganizations, employee stock ownership plans, and estate and gift tax planning and compliance matters.

ACKNOWLEDGEMENTS

The idea for this handbook was first discussed with Barbara Walters Price, Senior Vice President of Mercer Capital, in the summer of 2007. More likely than not, this book would not have been the end result of those conversations without a gentle push from Barbara to set the wheels in motion and begin outlining, researching, and ultimately drafting the book. Barbara brought a wealth of experience from several prior publications that helped to guide us through this process. For her belief and support of this project, we are extremely thankful.

A number of other colleagues also assisted with the development of this book, and we are very grateful for their contributions. We extend our thanks to everyone at Mercer Capital for encouraging, assisting, and providing the intellectual resources to draft and complete the book. Ken Patton, Laura Hoffmeister, and Kristin Beckman, three colleagues and fellow members of our Financial Institutions Group, served as contributing authors. We thank them for their commitment to the book and their wonderful contributions.

Three other people also gave significant contributions to the book. Maddie Gilman provided a diligent review of the book as well as a substantial portion of research for the recent changes in the banking industry and the government's response, which are covered in the Addendum. She is also a contributing author. Matthew Washburn worked tirelessly to create the design, layout, and graphics for the book, and we are especially grateful for his contributions. Charles Simmons worked diligently to research a number of the websites listed in the bibliography of the handbook and provided research into certain specific issues discussed in the handbook.

Our friends and family have also been sources of encouragement and support as the book came into being, and we would like to extend our thanks to them as well.

Lastly, we want to thank our clients. The origins of the handbook are rooted in a number of experiences with our clients and their boards over the years. From these experiences, we were able to learn valuable lessons that provided the basis for many of the topics discussed in this book. With this book, we hope to leverage these experiences and help other banks and their directors gain a better understanding of valuation issues and the potential impact of these issues on their banks. Additionally, several clients provided a review of the book and some valuable feedback. While reasons of confidentiality prevent us from mentioning them by name, their contributions were especially helpful.

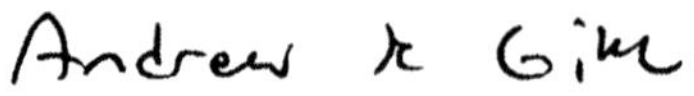

Andrew K. Gibbs, CFA, CPA/ABV

James D. Wilson, Jr.

TABLE OF CONTENTS

SECTION ONE

INTRODUCTION TO VALUATION

> I think a lot of modern day guitarists start off playing like Eddie van Halen, and they don't take the time to learn the basics.
>
> Lee Alvin
> *Musician*

Our objective in the first section of this book is to provide you with a general understanding of the basics of valuing financial institutions. Chapter 1 contains an overview of the valuation process covering such topics as when your financial institution might need a valuation, what to expect during the valuation process, and how to define the valuation. Chapters 2 and 3 provide a foundation for you to understand how a conclusion of value is derived and ascertain if the conclusion was determined reasonably. More specifically, Chapter 2 provides an overview of three core valuation concepts: the standard of value, the levels of value, and valuation approaches. Chapter 3 provides a brief discussion on the risks inherent to a bank that should be considered by an appraiser when valuing your financial institution.

CHAPTER 1

THE VALUATION PROCESS

Our discussion with bankers often begins with a simple question: "What is a business valuation?" The question is straightforward; however, it involves critical nuances that you should understand. Business valuation is defined in the American Society of Appraisers' *Business Valuation Standards* ("*ASA BV Standards*") as "the act or process of determining the value of a business or ownership interest therein."[1] In the context of financial institutions, business valuation is the process of determining the worth (value) of an interest (either a portion or the entirety) based upon due consideration of the relevant facts and circumstances as well as the exercise of judgment.

Business valuation professionals may perform differing scopes of work according to their professional standards. The concept of scope is important, since the scope of work has to match the intended use of the report. For this book we use the word "valuation" as a catch-all term for all scopes of work. The use of the term "appraisal" implies a more specific definition, which we define in a subsequent section.

WHEN MIGHT A FINANCIAL INSTITUTION NEED A BUSINESS VALUATION?

The question for most financial institutions is not if a valuation is necessary, but when it will be required. Even a relatively small financial institution is a substantial economic entity with transactional requirements similar to larger, publicly traded institutions. The following table outlines the types of valuation assignments that we frequently encounter with our banking clients.

Type of Valuation Assignment	When/Why in Bank Life?	Why is Appraisal Needed?
Periodic Independent Appraisal	Every couple of years or so for small banks; Every year for larger banks or banks with larger numbers of shareholders	Lifetime planning; Business planning; Board of director guidance; Being ready for unsolicited offers; etc.
Compensation & Employee Benefit Plans (Section 2)		
ESOPs	Employee benefits; Shareholder liquidity; To raise capital or acquire shares from existing shareholders	Independent valuation required by law; Financial advice for ESOP trustees
Stock Options	Employee benefits	Tax compliance and administration of the plans
Stock Transactions (Section 3)		
Charitable Gifts	When gifts are made	File appraisals with gift tax returns
Lifetime Gifts	Estate planning; Use annual exclusion to shift value to others to avoid estate taxation	File appraisals with gift tax returns
Estate Tax	Upon death	Document value of closely held shares in estate; File appraisals with estate tax returns
Raising Capital	When a bank needs to raise capital; Shareholders seek liquidity; Going public	Knowledge of pricing factors; Negotiation with underwriters
Buy-Sell Agreements	Any time when there are multiple shareholders; To ensure maintenance of Subchapter S status	Provide independent basis for buy-sell price; Establish and update buy-sell agreement values
Buy-Sell Agreements - Life Insurance	When purchasing insurance for buy-sell agreements	Avoid excess coverage; Ensure adequate coverage
Strategic Alternatives (Section 4)		
Mergers	Bank is growing; Access to capital; Liquidity for investors	Set stock exchange ratios; Independent opinion of value
Acquisitions	Bank is growing and/or desires to enter attractive market	Appraise equity for sale; Stock exchange ratios; Fairness opinions; Value the target to assist with initial offer and negotiations
Sale	Prior to sale	Analyze strategic alternatives; Have knowledge of bank; Use as a negotiating tool
Fairness Opinions	Sale or other major corporate transaction	Protect rights of minority shareholders (and interests of the board of directors)

Type of Valuation Assignment	When/Why in Bank Life?	Why is Appraisal Needed?
Financial Reporting (Section 5)		
Core Deposit Valuation	Following acquisitions	Allocate value to identifiable intangible assets
Securities Portfolio Valuation	Investment in illiquid securities; Periods of market volatility	To determine fair value of securities portfolio and whether "other than temporary" impairment may exist
Loan Portfolio Valuation	Following acquisitions	To determine fair value of loans held-for-sale or loans held-for-investment for footnote disclosure in audited financial statements
Goodwill Impairment Testing	Years following an acquisition	To determine the fair value of the reporting unit for purposes of performing Step 1 of the goodwill impairment test prescribed in SFAS 142
Share-Based Compensation	If stock options or other share-based compensation is used as employee compensation	To determine compensation expense for accounting purposes and the value of options granted for compensation purposes
Statutory & Legal Concepts (Section 6)		
Shareholder Disputes	They happen unexpectedly	Independent valuations help settle disputes over value; Often required in dissenting shareholder cases
Minority Shareholder Squeeze-Outs	Subchapter S election; Reverse stock splits; Going private transaction; Eliminate minority positions	Independent valuations help settle disputes over value; Often required in dissenting shareholder cases
Divorce	When closely held stock is in marital estate	Ensure fair value; Prepare for trial; Arbitrate value

TYPES OF WORK AN APPRAISER GENERALLY PROVIDES

According to the *ASA BV Standards*[2], there are generally three types of valuation assignments or scopes of work: appraisal, limited appraisal, and calculations. These three types of valuation assignments are described as follows.

» An **appraisal** is defined as "the act or process of determining the value of a business, business ownership interest, security, or intangible asset. The objective of an appraisal is to express *an unambiguous opinion* as to the value of a business, business ownership interest, or security, which opinion is supported by all procedures that the appraiser deems to be relevant to the valuation." (*emphasis added*)

» "The objective of a **limited appraisal** is to express *an estimate* as to the value of a business, business ownership interest, or security. The development of this estimate excludes some additional procedures that are required in an appraisal." *(emphasis added)*

» "The objective of **calculations** is to provide *an approximate indication* of value based upon the performance of limited procedures agreed upon by the appraiser and the client." *(emphasis added)*

The scope of work should agree with the intended use of the report. The failure to do so can lessen the credibility of the conclusion. We include a chart in Chapter 2 that shows the most common scope of work (appraisal, limited appraisal, and calculations) for different types of assignments.

SELECTING AN APPRAISER

Regardless of the reason your bank needs a valuation, one of the most critical decisions is the selection of the appraiser. When selecting an appraiser, defining the valuation assignment properly is vitally important, and you should consider a variety of factors, including experience, training, background, longevity in business, independence, and reputation. While fees are important to everyone, they should not be a primary consideration in your choice. The following list includes what we consider to be the primary questions to ask each appraiser prior to selection.

» Do you perform business valuations on a full-time basis?

» How many valuations has your firm performed over its history? How many annually? How many full-time appraisers are on your staff?

» Do you have a dedicated group of appraisers focused on the valuation of financial institutions? If so, how many appraisers are primarily focused on financial institutions?

» How many valuations of financial institutions has your firm performed? How many annually? How many valuation assignments has your firm performed that are similar to the assignment requested by the bank (ESOPs, estate tax, transaction advisory, statutory fair value, financial statement reporting, etc.)?

» Are your senior professionals members of professional organizations such as the Business Valuation discipline of the ASA, the CFA Institute, or other recognized professional groups?

» Have your professionals taught any valuation courses, spoken on valuation topics or published any articles or books on business valuation topics for financial institutions? If so, can you provide a list?

» Will you provide a list of references?

» Do you have access to the more prominent data sources such as Standard & Poor's, SNL Financial, *American Banker*, Ibbotson, or resources of similar quality?

» What is your litigation experience with financial institutions?

» Have you performed valuations of financial institutions for any governmental agencies (the Internal Revenue Service, the Department of Labor, etc.)?

UNDERSTANDING THE VALUATION PROCESS

While the steps for each assignment may vary depending upon the scope of work provided (appraisal, limited appraisal, or calculations), the appraisal assignment typically progresses in the following steps.

1. **Define the Valuation Assignment** – According to the *ASA BV Standards*, the appraiser should identify and define each of the following: 1) the business, business ownership interest, or security to be valued; 2) the effective date of the appraisal; 3) the standard of value; and, 4) the purpose and intended use of the valuation. Additionally, the nature and scope of work (appraisal, limited appraisal, or calculations) should also be defined.[3] Generally, this part of the process includes discussion between a number of parties, including the appraiser, the client, and the client's tax and legal counsel, when appropriate.

   One important component not to overlook is specifying the effective date of the appraisal, which appraisers typically refer to this date as the "as of" date of the valuation. Once this date is established, appraisers rely upon information that is (or was) reasonably available to conduct due diligence for the valuation assignment. For banks, appraisals are typically based upon the most recent quarterly financial statements that would have been available prior to the valuation date. For example, an appraisal with an effective date of July 15, 2008 would rely primarily upon June 30, 2008 financial data. In certain situations, a valuation is needed at an effective date in the distant past, which requires the appraiser to exercise judgment as to what would have been available at that particular time. This occurs often in valuations to be used for estate tax or litigation purposes.

2. **Gather Information** – At this point in the process, the appraiser gathers and analyzes the information required to perform a valuation appropriate to the scope of work.[4] While valuing financial institutions has some advantages in the information gathering process due to the amount of publicly available financial information, an appraiser typically sends an information request to the client for additional items that are not publicly available, such as board reports, asset/liability management reports, shareholder agreements, lists of graded loans and loan loss reserve

adequacy calculations, securities portfolio inventories, and other documentation deemed necessary for the specific engagement.

3. **Conduct On-Site Visit** – The on-site visit provides the analyst with an opportunity to develop an understanding of how the subject financial institution operates and to integrate many sources of information about a particular bank into a logical framework. Specific objectives of the visit include reviewing details of documents previously provided, developing an opinion of the local economy based on observation, developing an impression of management and their ability to achieve anticipated operating results, and identifying factors or trends that can be expected to influence future performance. From time to time, the appraiser may conduct the interview by telephone if circumstances warrant it.

4. **Draft the Report** – At this point, the ball is in the appraiser's court and the appraiser works to prepare the valuation analysis and draft of the valuation report.

5. **Issue the Draft Report to Client and Client Review** – The client receives a copy of the draft report and is given the opportunity to review and question the appraiser's analysis. As a user of a valuation report, providing an adequate review to evaluate the appraiser's assumptions and confirm the accuracy of factual statements is important.

6. **Finalize the Valuation Report** – Once the client, their advisors, and any other interested parties have had a chance to review the report and pose any questions or comments regarding the draft to the appraiser, the appraiser issues the final report.

While the steps outlined above are subject to change depending upon the circumstances of each valuation assignment and the specific appraisal firm engaged, they provide a general outline of the steps involved and what to expect should you retain a valuation professional to perform a valuation.

WHEN TO ENGAGE THE APPRAISER

If you determine that a valuation assignment is needed, it is always important engaging the appraiser sooner rather than later. Generally, the timetable for gathering the necessary factual information from a client, the on-site visit, and the preparation and rendering of any draft and final report should be agreed upon between the appraiser and the client prior to starting the valuation process. At Mercer Capital, we strive to issue a draft of the report approximately 30 days following the completion of the on-site visit.

CHAPTER 2

CORE VALUATION CONCEPTS

Chapter 1 provides an overview of the valuation process, stressing the importance of defining the valuation assignment. Once the valuation has been appropriately defined, the appraiser should then be able to determine a valuation conclusion and deliver a draft report. The next two chapters provide the foundation to understand how the conclusion of value is derived and determine if the conclusion is reasonable. The three concepts discussed in this chapter are the standard of value, the levels of value, and the valuation approaches most commonly used for financial institutions.

THE STANDARD OF VALUE

It is vital for appraisers, clients, boards of directors, and other users of valuation reports to understand the standard of value in an appraisal. The appropriate standard of value should be determined at the outset of the valuation engagement and should be based upon discussion with the appropriate legal, tax, and valuation professionals. The *ASA BV Standards* define the standard of value as "the identification of the type of value being used in a specific engagement; e.g., fair market value, fair value, investment value."[5] The selection of the standard of value drives the application of valuation methods; therefore, it is essential that the proper standard be selected for the transaction you are contemplating. Two of the most common standards of value, fair market value and fair value, are subsequently discussed.

Fair Market Value

Fair market value is the most widely known standard of value and is applicable to almost all federal and state tax valuation matters. Fair market value has been defined in numerous court cases, as well as in Internal Revenue Service Ruling 59-60. Fair market value is defined by the American Society of Appraisers as:

> "The price, expressed in terms of cash equivalents, at which property would change hands between a hypothetical willing and able buyer and a hypothetical willing and able seller, acting at arm's length in an open and unrestricted market, when neither is under compulsion to buy or sell and when both have reasonable knowledge of the relevant facts."[6]

Several important points to note regarding the definition of fair market value are listed below.

» **The Willing Seller and the Willing Buyer.** Both are hypothetical parties. Each is assumed to be well-informed about the subject interest and the market context in which it might be transacted.

» **Arm's Length.** Fair market value assumes willing, financially capable, and informed buyers and sellers, neither of whom is related or acting under any compulsion.

» **Cash Equivalent Value.** Fair market value assumes that any deferred payments in transactions are converted to cash equivalent amounts.[7]

» **Importance of Conditions in Existence at the Valuation Date.** Both internal conditions (financial health of subject bank, credit quality, etc.) and external conditions (state of stock markets, the relevant local, regional, or national economy, and industry conditions) must be determined by investigation and will influence the conclusion of value. From the point of view of fair market value, these conditions and their future outlook "are what they are" as of any specific valuation date. For example, valuing banks during periods when banks were trading at discounts to book value (such as the early 1980s or 2008) provided lower valuation conclusions for banks of equivalent performance than market conditions in the late 1980s and late 1990s.

» **Focus on the Critical Three - Common Sense, Informed Judgment, and Reasonableness.** Revenue Ruling 59-60 states: "A sound valuation will be based upon all the relevant facts, but the elements of common sense, informed judgment and reasonableness must enter into the process of weighing those facts and determining their aggregate significance."[8] Therefore, appraisers refer to common sense, informed judgment, and reasonableness as "the critical three" factors that must be present in every appraisal.

Fair Value

The term fair value is often used as a standard of value in two types of valuation assignments. Fair value is either used as the standard of value for certain transactions that trigger dissenters' rights, or as the standard of value for financial statement reporting purposes. The following discussion relates to fair value in the context of transactions involving dissenters' rights. Fair value as a standard of value for financial statement reporting purposes is defined in the relevant accounting standards, and is discussed in greater detail in Section Five, Chapter 13: Fair Value Accounting.

Statutory fair value is often applicable to cases involving appraisal rights of minority shareholders typically arising from certain corporate actions covered by various state statutes. Common corporate actions triggering dissenters' rights include reorganizations or recapitalizations. Fair value is generally defined by judicial interpretation of the relevant statute in that particular state. There are a number of conflicts in the various legal jurisdictions regarding the interpretation of fair value statutes.

Common questions that arise include:

» What is the appropriate level of value (as described more fully in a subsequent section of this chapter) to determine fair value in the particular jurisdiction?

» Is fair value the same thing as fair market value?

- Are marketability and/or minority interest discounts appropriate?
- Should synergies be considered?

When a matter involving fair value emerges, valuation experts must be aware of the specific state law and any applicable dissenting minority shareholder case law in the state of incorporation of the subject financial institution. Additionally, banks and their directors should be aware of applicable statutes and case law when engaging in transactions that could trigger dissenters' rights.

THE TRADITIONAL LEVELS OF VALUE

Valuation theory suggests that there are three general levels of value applicable to a business or business ownership interest. Many writers parse these ideas more precisely. Our objective is not to delineate or explain every potential refinement to the levels of value chart; instead our purpose is to inform you of the concepts and their importance to every valuation assignment. For purposes of perspective, we define the three traditional levels of value as:

- **Controlling interest basis** refers to the value of the enterprise as a whole.
- **Marketable minority interest basis** refers to the value of a minority interest, lacking control, but enjoying the benefit of liquidity as if it were freely tradeable in an active market.
- **Nonmarketable minority interest basis** refers to the value of a minority interest, lacking both control and market liquidity.

The following traditional levels of value chart shows the relationship between the three levels of value and demonstrates how the indications of value are obtained at each level of value.

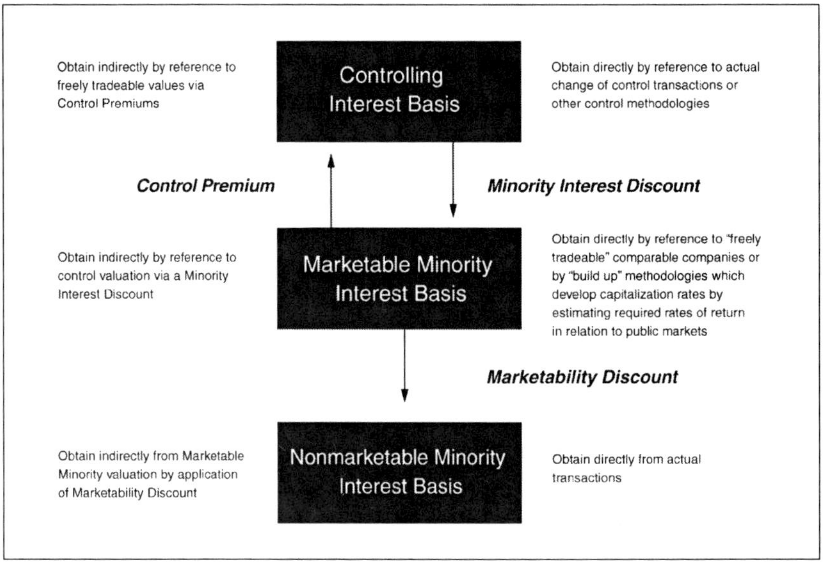

Controlling Interest Level of Value

The highest level of value is called the controlling interest level of value. Controlling interest indications of value are commonly obtained directly by reference to actual change of control transactions using the merger and acquisition method, which is described in the discussion of valuation approaches later in this chapter. Additionally, controlling interest indications of value can be obtained indirectly by reference to freely tradable values using a control premium.

Analogous to the marketability discount, the control premium is the difference between the value of a subject interest that exercises control over the company and the value of that same interest lacking control (but enjoying marketability). In practice, the control premium is generally expressed as a percentage of the marketable minority value. When the difference is expressed as a percentage of the controlling interest value, it is referred to as a minority interest discount. Both the concept of the control premium and that of the minority interest discount have been addressed in numerous studies by appraisal professionals and by the various courts.[9]

Many valuation experts further subdivide the controlling interest level of value into financial control and strategic control. We define financial control and strategic control as:

» **Strategic controlling interest basis** refers to the value of the enterprise as a whole, incorporating the strategic intent that may motivate particular buyers and the expected synergies that may result from an acquisition.

» **Financial controlling interest basis** refers to the value of the enterprise excluding any revenue and expense synergies that may accrue to a strategic buyer. This level of value is viewed from the perspective of a financial buyer, who may expect to benefit by improving the enterprise's cash flow and its capital structure but not through any operating synergies that may be available to a strategic buyer.

If adjusted, the levels of value chart would look something like this.

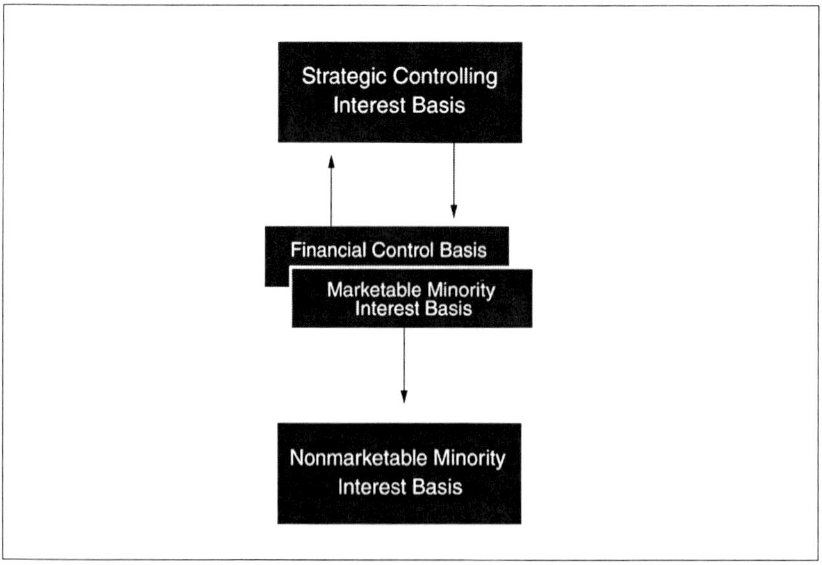

Observing the differential between the financial controlling interest level of value and the strategic controlling interest level of value at a specific time in a particular industry can be difficult for a variety of reasons. Generally, a conclusion of value at the strategic controlling interest level of value results in a conclusion of value greater than financial control. However, a preponderance of financial buyers in a given industry can result in competitive bidding and the acceptance of lower returns by an individual financial buyer, which may increase prices paid by financial buyers to a level comparable to the prices offered and/or paid by strategic buyers.

Marketable Minority Interest Level of Value

The marketable minority interest level of value is typically the reference point for which the other levels are described. Indications of value on a marketable minority interest basis are often obtained by reference to valuation multiples of comparable publicly traded companies using the guideline public company method, which is described in the discussion of valuation approaches later in this chapter. Marketable minority interest indications of value can also be obtained directly by using a build-up methodology, which develops capitalization rates by estimating required rates of return in relation to public markets, or indirectly by reference to a control valuation via the application of a minority interest discount to reflect the lack of control.

Nonmarketable Minority Interest Level of Value

The nonmarketable minority interest value is typically derived by determining value at the marketable minority interest level of value and then applying a discount for lack of marketability. The ASA defines a discount for lack of marketability as "an amount or percentage deducted from the value of an ownership interest to reflect the relative absence of marketability."[10] Thus, a marketable minority interest would be worth more than a nonmarketable minority interest that is identical in all other respects, and the difference between the two (the marketability discount) is due to the inherent risk of holding an illiquid asset. In practice, this discount is generally expressed as a percentage of the marketable minority value and can range from very small (5%-10%) to large (60%-70% or more).

Historically, analysts have quantified the marketability discount using either a market approach or an income approach. The valuation methods relied upon within the market approach are commonly referred to collectively as "benchmark analysis." Benchmark analysis considers data from 1) restricted stock transactions, 2) pre-IPO studies, and 3) decisions rendered in court cases. In our experience, the use of a market approach to value a nonmarketable interest is limited by the quality and relevance of available data.

Since the mid-1990s, alternative methodologies have been developed within the income approach to analyze the marketability discount. These methods have focused on valuing the benefits accruing to the owner of an illiquid interest consistent with the manner in which businesses are valued using a discounted cash flow ("DCF") model. One such DCF model is the Quantitative Marketability Discount Model ("QMDM") which Mercer Capital began using in the mid-1990s.

The QMDM is a shareholder-level discounted cash flow model designed to help the appraiser derive and explain a reasonable and transparent conclusion based upon the facts and circumstances of each case. The QMDM is based upon a set of assumptions, which are comparable to the necessary components of any DCF model.

For additional perspective, consider the hypothetical case of the following two banks.

	Farmers Bank	Peoples Bank
Expected Growth	Growing slowly	Growing rapidly
Interim Benefits	No dividend	Dividend
Expected Holding Period	5-10 years	1-3 years
Restrictions on Transfer	Yes	No

Considering the factors above, an appraiser would typically determine that a higher marketability discount is appropriate for Farmers Bank (all else equal) than Peoples Bank. An investor in Farmers Bank would face greater restrictions on selling the stock, has a longer expected holding period, and receives lower interim benefits in the form of slower growth and no dividend relative to the investor in Peoples Bank.

Summary

Two oft-forgotten concepts related to valuation discounts and premiums are also important. The first is that no premium or discount has any meaning apart from a well-defined base value to which it is applied. A marketability discount or a control premium has no meaning apart from a marketable minority interest value to which it is applied. In the same way, a minority interest discount is meaningless in the absence of a determination of value on a controlling interest basis. The second is that valuation discounts and premiums are ultimately outputs of, not inputs to, a well-reasoned valuation. Discounts and premiums are shorthand ways of describing differences in value attributable to economic differences between related subject interests. They are not, and cannot be treated as, the source of valuation differences. Investors evaluate the worth of a particular interest by reference to the expected cash flows, growth potential, and risk characteristics of that interest. Varying expectations among interests lead to discounts and premiums.

Confusion between the appraiser and the user of the valuation over the proper level of value can result in a serious misunderstanding, and ultimately, an inappropriately high or low conclusion of value. Thus, both business appraisers and the parties using the valuations should be aware of the correct basis of valuation (i.e., controlling, marketable minority, or nonmarketable minority).

Below we provide a chart outlining some examples of the types of valuations performed at each level of value.

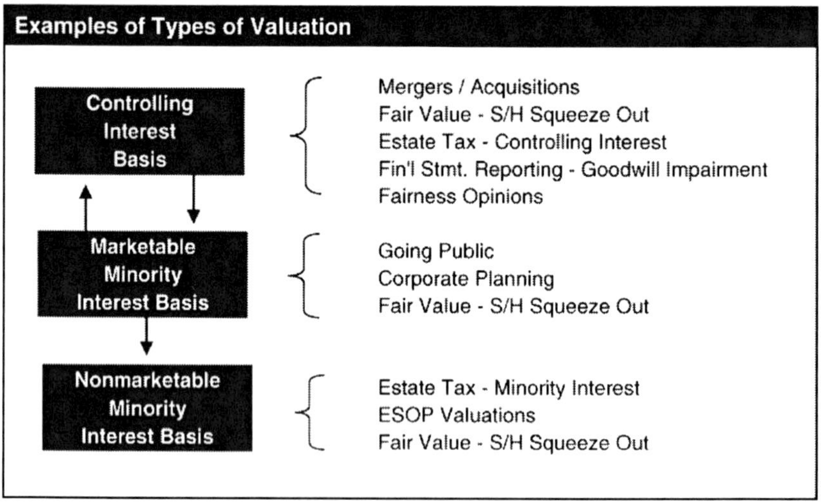

VALUATION APPROACHES

The process of creating a valuation means consideration of various ways of measuring value. Since Mercer Capital adheres primarily to the *ASA BV Standards,* we use its terminology. The ASA recognizes three general approaches to valuation. Within each approach, the appraiser may apply various methods. The valuation methods used are considered by the appraiser to be those most appropriate to the valuation.

Asset Approach

The *ASA BV Standards* define the asset approach as "a general way of determining a value indication of a business, business ownership interest, security, or intangible asset using one or more methods based on the value of the assets net of liabilities."[11] Asset-based valuation methods include those methods that seek to write up (or down) or otherwise adjust the various tangible and/or intangible assets of an enterprise.

Within the asset approach, a common method used for valuing a financial institution is the net asset value method. The net asset value method develops a valuation indication in the context of a going concern by adjusting the reported book values of a subject bank's assets to their market values and subtracting its liabilities (adjusted to market value, if appropriate). The indicated value should not be interpreted as an estimate of liquidation value.

Income Approach

The *ASA BV Standards* define the income approach as "a general way of determining a value indication of a business, business ownership interest, security, or intangible asset by using one or more methods that convert anticipated economic benefits into a present single amount.[12] Valuation methods under the income approach include those methods that provide for the direct capitalization of earnings estimates, as well as valuation methods calling for the forecasting of future benefits (earnings or cash flows) and then discounting those benefits to the present at an appropriate discount rate. One of the most common methods used to value financial institutions within the income approach is the discounted future benefits method, which relies upon a projection of a future stream of benefits, the present value of which represents the indication of value of the subject bank.

Market Approach

The *ASA BV Standards* define the market approach as "a general way of determining a value indication of a business, business ownership interest, security or intangible asset by using one or more methods that compare the subject to similar businesses, business ownership interests, securities or intangible assets that have been sold."[13]

Within the market approach, the most common methods utilized are:

» **The Transactions Method.** The transactions method develops an indication of value based upon consideration of actual transactions in the stock of a subject entity. Transactions are reviewed to determine if they have occurred at arm's length, with a reasonable degree of frequency, and within a reasonable period of time relative to the valuation date. Finally, the transactions should be of a similar level of value (i.e., a limited number of transactions involving a small number of shares would generally be inappropriate for a controlling interest valuation). Inferences about current value can sometimes be drawn, even if there is only a limited market for the shares and relatively few transactions occur.

» **The Guideline Public Company Method.**[14] The guideline public company method develops an indication of value based upon pricing multiples of guideline companies. When involving banks, guideline companies are most often publicly traded financial institutions that provide a reasonable basis for comparison to the investment characteristics of the subject bank. Sifting through the hundreds of publicly traded banks in the United States, appraisers evaluate comparability on the basis of several measures, most notably asset size, geographic location, asset quality, and profitability. The most commonly used version develops a price/earnings ("P/E") ratio with which to capitalize net income. If the public company group is sufficiently homogeneous with respect to the companies selected and their financial performance, analysts may begin the analysis by calculating an average or median P/E ratio as representative of the group or subdivide the group by other means. If the analyst determines that certain fundamental differences exist between the guideline companies and the subject bank, then the analyst may adjust the median or average multiples to account for these differences. Other relevant valuation indicators for financial institutions may include price/book value and price/tangible book value.

» **The Guidelines Transactions Method.**[15] Also referred to as the merger and acquisition method, the guideline transactions method develops an indication of value based on change of control transactions involving target banks with investment characteristics comparable to the subject bank. Transactions are screened to include only those that occurred within a reasonable period of time proximate to the effective date of the valuation and involve target banks with comparable qualities, including asset size, asset quality, geographic location, and profitability. The most commonly used version develops a P/E ratio that is used to capitalize net income. Other relevant valuation indicators for the banking industry may include price/book value, price/tangible book value, and the premium to core deposits.

DEFINING THE VALUATION ASSIGNMENT

The following chart serves as a guide to future chapters and a reference to help you structure a valuation assignment for your bank. A note of caution: the chart is only a guide. Always obtain appropriate legal advice for your specific need before you formalize an engagement. In the remaining chapters, we discuss in further detail each type of valuation assignment shown in the chart.

Ch	Type of Valuation	Client	Business Name/ Asset Description	Business Interest Under Consideration	Standard of Value	Level of Value	Effective Date of Valuation	Purpose and Intended Use	Type of Report / Scope of Work
4	**Employee Benefit Plans**	Trustee of the Plan	Bank / BHC	Typically, a minority interest in the bank's stock	Fair Market Value	Typically nonmarketable minority interest basis	Typically at year-end	Plan administration	Appraisal
5	**Stock Options, Restricted Stock, & Stock Appreciation Rights**	Bank / BHC	Bank / BHC	Typically, a minority interest in the bank's stock that is underlying the stock-based compensation	Fair Market Value	Typically nonmarketable minority interest basis	Dependent upon bank policy or preference; Check Section 409A requirements when issued	Tax compliance and administration of the plans	Appraisal
6	**Estate & Gift Tax Issues**	Executor / Benefeciary of Estate / Gift	Bank / BHC	Varies depending upon size of interest	Fair Market Value	Varies depending upon size of interest	Estate: Date of death or alternate date (6 months following date of death); Gift: Date of gift	Estate or gift tax compliance	Appraisal
7	**Raising Capital**	Bank / BHC / Investor	Bank / BHC	Depends on nature of the transaction and form of capital being raised	Fair Market Value	Depends on nature of the transaction	Typically current date (close to date of issuance)	Used in conjunction with the issuance and sale of security	Varies depending upon assignment and nature of transaction
8	**Buy-Sell Agreements**	Should be specified in buy-sell agreement							
9	**Mergers & Acquisitions**	Bank / BHC	Bank / BHC	Bank / BHC	Varies	Controlling interest	As of a current date	Review of target's/selling bank's financial performance and derivation of target's/subject bank's value	Calculations, limited appraisal, or appraisal
10	**Fairness Opinions**	Attorney / Board of Dir. / Bank / BHC	Bank / BHC	Bank / BHC	N/A	N/A	N/A	To review the proposed transaction and provide the bank with an opinion as to the fairness of the proposed transaction from a financial point of view	Fairness opinion letter and potentially a fairness opinion memorandum that supports the fairness opinion
11	**Capital Gains & Dividends**	Varies depending upon assignment							

Ch.	Type of Valuation	Client	Business Name/ Asset Description	Business Interest Under Consideration	Standard of Value	Level of Value	Effective Date of Valuation	Purpose and Intended Use	Type of Report / Scope of Work
12	**Sub-Chapter S Conversions**	Attorney / Bank / BHC	Bank / BHC	Varies depending upon number of shares to be repurchased	Fair Value, as defined under applicable state law	Typically determined based upon discussions with legal counsel	Typically the date that the transaction occurs	Used in conjunction with the transactions required to repurchase shares from certain shareholders of the bank to potentially elect Subchapter S status	Appraisal
13	**Securities Valuation**	Bank / BHC	Securities portfolio of acquired bank	N/A	Fair Value, as defined in SFAS 141R and SFAS 157	N/A	Typically closing date of the acquisition	Financial reporting under GAAP	Typically appraisal, but could also be calculations
13	**Loan Portfolio Valuation**	Bank / BHC	Loan portfolio of acquired bank	N/A	Fair Value, as defined in SFAS 141R and SFAS 157	N/A	Typically closing date of the acquisition	Financial reporting under GAAP	Typically appraisal, but could also be calculations
14	**Depositor Customer Relationships**	Bank / BHC	Depositor relationships of acquired bank	N/A	Fair Value, as defined in SFAS 141R and SFAS 157	N/A	Typically closing date of the acquisition	Financial reporting under GAAP	Typically appraisal, but could also be calculations
14	**Goodwill Impairment Test**	Bank / BHC	Reporting unit, such as a subsidiary bank, insurance or mortgage co., or other subsidiary	N/A	Fair Value, as defined in SFAS 142 or SFAS 157	Controlling interest	A date selected by management that should ordinarily be consistent from year to year	Determination of the fair value of the reporting unit for purposes of performing Step 1 of the goodwill impairment test prescribed by SFAS 142	Typically appraisal, but could also be calculations
15	**Share-Based Compensation**	Bank / BHC	Bank / BHC	N/A	Fair Value, as defined in SFAS 123R	N/A	Date the share-based compensation was issued	Financial reporting under GAAP	Typically calculations
16-18	**Litigated Matters**	Varies depending upon assignment, should be instructed by attorney							

CHAPTER 3

FINANCIAL MANAGEMENT & PERFORMANCE MEASUREMENT

A detailed discussion of all the key operating risks faced by banks is beyond the scope and intent of this book. We include this overview for one important reason: it provides a summary of risks that should be considered by your appraiser. Use it as a guide for evaluating the insight and thoroughness that was (or will be) applied in constructing the valuation analysis. If you do not see these items in the final valuation report, then you have reason to wonder if your appraiser had an appropriate understanding of your institution.

PRIMARY FINANCIAL RISKS

Banks act as intermediaries between customers seeking to lend funds (depositors) and customers requiring funds (borrowers). When acting as an intermediary, banks accept a certain measure of risk, and the appropriate management of these risks is necessary to create shareholder value. Before discussing how to measure performance, it is important to understand the risk framework within which banks operate.

Banks face three primary financial risks.

» **Credit Risk.** Credit risk is the potential that some of a bank's investments, in either loans or securities, may not be repaid according to their terms. Banks attempt to mitigate credit risk by, for instance, lending only a fraction of the collateral value, requiring guarantees, charging more for higher risk loans, or purchasing only government agency securities. Nevertheless, losses are inevitable, and banks that seek to avoid losses altogether may find themselves at the other end of the spectrum – taking too little risk. Credit risk should be monitored closely, given the leverage inherent in a bank's balance sheet, since $100 of equity often supports $1,250 or more of assets. Thus, problems with a relatively small proportion of a bank's loans could quickly jeopardize the entire equity account.

» **Interest Rate Risk.** Interest rate risk relates to changes in net interest income caused by changes in market interest rates. For instance, as interest rates decline, banks with significant floating rate loan portfolios may see the rates earned on their assets fall faster than their deposit rates, because time deposit rates only adjust when the CD matures. Interest rate risk is difficult to avoid altogether; thus, the focus is on managing this risk. Banks seek to avoid large swings in earnings or book value from interest rate changes but will take measures to position the balance sheet for expected changes in interest rates, such as emphasizing shorter term CDs when interest rates are forecast to decline.

» **Liquidity Risk.** Liquidity risk relates to the bank's ability to meet its obligations, such as commitments to fund loans or deposit withdrawals, in the ordinary course of business. As evidenced by the collapse of Bear Stearns and the "run" on Indy Mac in 2008, liquidity risk is highly important to financial institutions. Most liquidity strategies involve maintaining unpledged assets on the balance sheet or having access to various untapped sources of funds in the event that the unexpected occurs. Liquidity has its trade-offs, however. Maintaining a pool of liquid assets often involves forsaking the higher yields that could be earned on illiquid assets, like loans, for lower yielding, but highly liquid, securities investments.

If the preceding risks are inappropriately managed, the bank's capital could be jeopardized. To ensure the safety and soundness of the institution, regulators focus intently on the sufficiency of capital. Regulatory standards require certain amounts of capital in relation to the amount and type of assets held. Capital is basically shareholders' equity, minus intangible assets, plus additional components that meet certain specified criteria. These capital requirements effectively limit the amount of leverage that banks can utilize. Particularly for banks experiencing rapid growth, directors will need to ensure that an appropriate strategy exists to maintain compliance with capital requirements. On the other hand, it is possible for a bank to have too much capital. Capital well in excess of the regulatory requirements could be distributed to the shareholders for investment elsewhere, thereby enhancing the shareholders' returns.

BALANCE SHEET PERFORMANCE AND RISK MEASURES

The following lists some of the key financial measures from the balance sheet.

» **Loan/Deposit or Loan/Asset Ratios.** Banks with low loan/deposit ratios may be taking too little credit risk – meaning that the low risk tolerance is causing it to pass up opportunities that other banks willingly accept. This can lead to sub-optimal returns for shareholders. On the other hand, a high loan/deposit ratio suggests that a high proportion of the bank's assets are invested in illiquid loans, necessitating a greater focus on liquidity risk management.

» **Loan Portfolio Composition.** To reduce credit risk, banks seek to maintain loan portfolios that are diversified by, for instance, loan type and industry segment. If directors notice that growth is occurring disproportionately in one type of loan, then they may wish to inquire as to whether adequate controls are in place to manage any potential concentration.

» **Loan Loss Reserve.** Banks maintain loan loss reserves to cover probable loan losses in the portfolio. The adequacy of the reserve can be measured by evaluating ratios such as the loan loss reserve/total loans ratio or the loan loss reserve/non-performing loans ratio. A low ratio could infer greater risk and the loan loss reserve may be inadequate to cover any losses.

» **Non-Performing Assets.** To assess credit risk, banks monitor trends in past-due loans, internal loan gradings, among others. While an increase in past-due loans does not necessarily forecast greater future losses, it may necessitate enhanced monitoring by the board of directors.

INCOME STATEMENT PERFORMANCE MEASURES

The following lists some of the key financial measures from the income statement.

» **Net Interest Income.** Most of a bank's revenue comes from net interest income, which is simply the difference between interest income and interest expense. Changes in net interest income occur because of changes in either the amount or mix of earning assets or the spread between rates earned and rates paid. Various ways exist to calculate the spreads between rates earned and rates paid, such as the net spread or the net interest margin.

» **Non-Interest Income.** Non-interest income includes items such as deposit account service charges and mortgage banking income. Expanding non-interest income has been an area of great importance to bankers for years. One advantage of non-interest income is that it is often less sensitive to changes in interest rates than net interest income, thus creating some revenue diversification. To compare non-interest income across banks, directors can calculate the proportion of non-interest income to total assets or total revenues.

» **Non-Interest Expenses.** Like any business, the bank's goal is to grow its revenue (net interest income and non-interest income) faster than its operating expenses. In the short-run, investments in expansion initiatives like new branches could result in more rapid expense growth with the long-term goal that expense growth will drop below the rate of revenue growth as the expansion initiative bears fruit. Ratios used to compare expense trends include the ratio of operating expenses to assets and the ratio of operating expenses to revenue (the efficiency ratio). The efficiency ratio is one of the few ratios where a lower ratio is preferred to a higher one.

» **Loan Loss Provision.** The loan loss provision is the income statement charge to replenish or increase the loan loss reserve. While the loan loss provision may drop below net charge-offs for short periods of time, directors should not count on this trend persisting for any length of time.

» **Return on Equity.** The return on equity is net income divided by equity (use of average equity often occurs) and measures the return that the bank generates on its equity.

» **Return on Assets.** The return on assets is net income divided by total assets (use of average assets often occurs). This ratio measures the return that the bank generates on its assets. While this measure has its traditional popularity, it has some shortcomings versus the return on equity measure. For instance, a bank can increase its return on assets, other factors held constant, by retaining its earnings and increasing its equity. However, the return on equity would suffer, and shareholder value would be enhanced if the earnings were distributed to the shareholders. Thus, the return on equity has a more direct relationship with shareholder value than return on assets.

SECTION TWO

COMPENSATION & EMPLOYEE BENEFIT PLANS

Start with good people, lay out the rules, communicate with employees, motivate and reward them. If you do all those things effectively, you can't miss.

Lee Iacocca
Former President & CEO
Chrysler Corporation

This section provides an overview of several different types of employee benefit plans and compensation packages, and highlights a number of financial issues to consider in evaluating them. Chapter 4 discusses the basics of employee benefit plans, describes the primary professionals whose services help resolve the valuation issues associated with these plans, and lists common questions that we have received from clients over the years. Chapter 5 continues the theme of equity-based compensation and provides an overview of three types of equity incentive instruments: stock options, restricted stock, and stock appreciation rights. In addition to this brief overview, a comparison of each type of equity compensation instrument is provided.

CHAPTER 4

EMPLOYEE BENEFIT PLANS

Banks frequently find employee stock ownership to be an attractive benefit. This chapter focuses on three means to accomplish employee ownership: employee stock ownership plans ("ESOP"), 401(k) plans, and Individual Retirement Accounts ("IRA"). An ESOP is designed to invest primarily in employer securities, while a 401(k) and an IRA may invest in employer stock, but will most likely hold a wide variety of securities. Because many banks are not publicly traded, there are valuation issues for all three types of programs.

OVERVIEW

In addition to providing the obvious financial benefit to employees, a properly administered and sufficiently funded (either through direct contributions from the bank or from borrowed funds that will be repaid through future contributions) employee benefit plan can contribute to minority shareholder liquidity directly by making a limited market in a bank's shares. For example, existing shareholders can offer shares to the employee benefit plan, which can then make purchases for the benefit of the employee beneficiaries.

The employee benefit plan also contributes to minority shareholder liquidity indirectly. An employee benefit plan that makes regular purchases of existing shares can help establish the market price for a bank's shares and can encourage other shareholders to engage in transactions at the market price. Shareholders generally know that employee benefit plan share prices are established by independent appraisal, and arm's length transactions tend to occur at many banks at or near the appraised share values (if the appraisal firm and the appraisals have credibility over time).

Parties Involved In Addressing the Valuation Issues

Employee benefit plan design and administration is complex and requires the services of a number of professionals. All three types of benefit plans have some commonality to their components.

» **Trustee** – The trustee acts as a fiduciary for the best interest of the plan participant. The trustee may be very active in an ESOP, but less so in a 401(k). The IRA is directed by the owner of the account. In the context of an ESOP, the trustee is responsible for the purchase of employer securities and the proper maintenance and administration of the plan. When dealing with closely held securities, the trustee has a heightened level of responsibility. With respect to any plan which requires an appraisal, the trustee must select the appraiser and approve the conclusion of value for securities held by the plan.

» **Administrator** – The administrator is responsible for record keeping and may also assist with tax filings and maintenance of plan documents.

» **Plan Sponsor** – The plan sponsor is typically the company.

» **Administrative Committee** – An administrative committee (known by a variety of names) is often formed to assist the plan administrator and trustee with various duties associated with the routine administration of the plan.

» **Attorney or Plan Designer** – The attorney works with the plan sponsor, administrative committee, and trustee to design the plan and create the documents necessary to implement it.

» **Fund Manager** – An investment manager may be utilized to invest funds held in the plan, primarily in the public securities markets.

» **Financial Advisor** – The financial advisor may assist the trustee in determining the feasibility of a plan or the fairness of transactions engaged in by the plan from a financial point of view.

» **Appraiser** – The appraiser provides the independent appraisal necessary to implement and administer the plan. (See Chapter 1, which discusses the scope of work by the appraiser. The use of the term "appraisal" is very specific in this context). The pricing of publicly traded securities by the plan administrator and/or fund manager is straightforward.

Who Regulates These Types of Benefit Plans?

The primary regulator of these types of employee benefit plans is the Department of Labor ("DOL"), which draws its authority from the Employee Retirement Income Security Act of 1974 ("ERISA"). Secondarily, the Internal Revenue Service has authority to review the activities of the plan because income tax deductions may be taken in many cases.

FINANCIAL ISSUES

The implementation of a new ESOP, annual valuation, or a change in share ownership prompts many questions. The plan's investment in employer securities creates a different level of complexity than that found in the typical 401(k) and IRA. As such, expert advice is needed often to resolve many issues, some of which are discussed below.

» **What are the phases of an ESOP valuation assignment?** For a new plan, the appraiser may be asked to do some type of preliminary determination of value in order to help assess the feasibility and attractiveness of a plan. The appraiser and the client (typically an administrative committee) agree to calculations (see scope of work discussion in Chapter 1) in order for the committee to have a baseline value. If a decision is made to proceed, then the appraiser renders an appraisal upon which the transaction can occur. For existing plans, the appraisal may be rendered annually, or as of the date of a significant transaction.

» **Has the DOL issued rules which govern the valuation of securities in an ESOP?** Many people are surprised to find that the answer is "no." An effort was made in 1988 to do so, but the rules were never finalized and were ultimately withdrawn. Since there are limited formal rules for construction of the appraisal, the ESOP and valuation community have taken steps to informally create them.

» **How often should an appraisal be obtained?** Due to an IRS rule, if the plan is leveraged, it must be valued annually. As an informal rule of practice (unsupported by any formal rule), the appraisal is generally valid for 60 days. If a significant event occurs in the interim, then the trustee might want to consider an update within the 60-day window. If a major transaction is occurring and a delay occurs, then the trustee may want to get a "take-down letter," which addresses whether the initial analysis is still valid as of the closing of the transaction. Use common sense here. If a reasonable person thinks that the appraisal should be as of a current date, then one should probably be obtained.

» **Does the use of leverage create complexity and misunderstanding?** Yes, it does in a variety of ways. First, if the portion of stock purchased is financed with debt, the transaction almost certainly will not create capital, since *American Institute of Certified Public Accountants Statement of Position 93-6* generally does not permit it. You should review this accounting pronouncement with your auditors very carefully before implementing a leveraged plan. Second, the value of the stock may fall after the leveraged plan is implemented. Third, the use of leverage can create dilution, which lowers value.

» **Why might the stock go down in value with the use of leverage?** An ESOP can engage in a minority interest (less than 50%) or controlling interest (more than 50%) leveraged transaction. When debt is involved, there is the expectation that it will be paid from contributions to the ESOP and possibly distributions (which are made to all shares). As a matter of common practice, most ESOP appraisers treat the debt and contributions in a minority interest transaction as an increase in compensation. Hence, costs rise and value falls, with all other things being equal. Value will rise over time as the debt is paid; however, ongoing contributions to the ESOP will continue to reduce earnings. In a control transaction, many appraisers treat the debt as though it were similar to an externally financed stock acquisition. This is appropriate because the controlling shareholder can sell the company and pay the debt. On rare occasions, the debt can be paid from distributions, therefore no reduction in the stock value occurs. In any case, be clear as to how the treatment of the debt will affect the stock value post transaction before you act, and be clear about how "mainstream" your appraiser's views are on this topic.

» **Can I sell a minority interest in my bank to the ESOP based upon a pro rata controlling interest price?** More than likely, the answer is "no." Since the DOL has long frowned on it, you should have expert legal and valuation advice if you believe this can be done in your specific case.

» **How is the discount for lack of marketability treated?** Appraisers often reduce the discount for lack of marketability if the ESOP plan document contains a "put" provision that is legally enforceable and financially viable. The put clause allows the participant to put the stock to the plan, to the employer, or both. As a result, discounts for lack of marketability are frequently seen in the range of 5% to 15% for securities which otherwise may have higher discounts based upon the liquidity of the stock absent the terms of the plan. An appraiser can apply a different discount for lack of marketability to stock inside an ESOP than to shares outside the plan.

» **What is an emerging liability and why is it important?** Stated simply, an emerging liability is the obligation of the plan or the employer to repurchase shares in the plan. The amount of the liability is a function of the value of the stock. Since repurchasing stock takes money, the repurchase of shares in a mature ESOP is often in conflict with other financial needs of the business, such as funds needed for expansion. The emerging liability is rarely an issue in new plans and may not be an issue for many years. Keep one thing in mind – treatment of the emerging liability can be a delicate issue. You cannot use it to unduly reduce the value of the stock and solve the cash flow problem of a mature ESOP.

» **When do we need a fairness opinion?** In the context of an ESOP, the trustee may desire a fairness opinion to seek greater comfort since it may have conflicts of interest, the transaction will be complicated, and numerous parties will review it. In any event, look to your legal counsel and financial advisor for direction. Fairness opinions are discussed in greater detail in Chapter 10.

» **What is dilution and why does it occur?** Dilution is a reduction in the fair market value per share, which occurs when there is an increase in the number of shares without an immediate, offsetting increase in value due to higher earnings or more capital. In the context of an ESOP, it occurs when: 1) shares are contributed to the plan and a tax deduction is taken for the fair market value of those shares; or, 2) newly issued shares are purchased by the plan and the purchase is financed with debt. Dilution is considered in the determination of fair market value at the time of the appraisal and should not be confused with the decline in value, which sometimes occurs when existing shares are purchased with debt. Dilution is encountered most frequently when a bank is doing a new stock offering and wants to include the ESOP in the transaction. The difficulty arises when the ESOP must purchase its stock with debt.

» **Does an ESOP appraisal have a low or high level of risk to all the parties?** Interestingly, the level of risk can be high. An appraisal is not a commodity with a common understanding of what "it" is. You are reliant on the quality of the provider and his or her ability to defend the appraisal to the DOL or plan participants. Regulatory scrutiny can be high and participant-initiated litigation is not uncommon.

CHAPTER 5

STOCK OPTIONS, RESTRICTED STOCK, & STOCK APPRECIATION RIGHTS

In addition to employee benefit plans, several other equity incentive instruments are often considered by banks. This chapter provides a brief introduction and comparison of three different types of equity incentive instruments: stock options, restricted stock, and stock appreciation rights.

OVERVIEW

Stock Options

Stock options give the holder the right to purchase a specific number of shares at some point in the future at a pre-determined price. Typically, a bank grants options with a vesting period, meaning the option holder may only purchase a certain portion of the total shares granted in any given time period. Options generally have an expiration date (for example, ten years from the date of the grant), and any options not exercised prior to the expiration date are terminated. Options are granted in two forms.

» **Nonqualified Stock Options ("NQOs")** are the simplest type of option and require the holder to pay income tax on the difference between the value of the underlying stock and the strike price at the time the option is exercised. The issuing company receives a corresponding tax deduction when the holder exercises a NQO. NQOs are used typically in broad-based employee plans, as they allow the issuer to avoid conforming to the more rigorous standards of incentive stock options.

» **Incentive Stock Options ("ISOs")** allow the holder to defer taxation until the shares granted with the option exercise are sold or transferred, and gains are taxed at capital gains rates rather than ordinary income tax levels.[16] An ISO loses its favorable tax treatment for the holder when a "disqualifying disposition" (i.e., a sale or transfer within two years of the grant or one year after exercise) occurs, which requires the holder to report the gain as ordinary income in the year of the disposition. However, the issuing bank may not deduct the related compensation expense for tax purposes. ISOs may be issued only to employees (in other words, non-employee directors may not be issued ISOs).

Restricted Stock

Restricted stock represents an outright grant of shares with restrictions on the sale, transfer, and/or pledging of the shares for a specified period of time. Like stock options, restricted stock typically vests in stages. Upon vesting, restricted stock is treated as compensation, and any difference between the market value at the date of termination and any subsequent change in value is treated as a capital gain or loss. Although stock options historically have been the equity incentive instrument of choice, restricted stock has increased in popularity. Benefits to restricted stock include the eligibility for dividends, even during the restricted period, and the holder is not required to pay for the stock as the shares are awarded to the employee directly.

Additional advantages of restricted stock include the ability of the holder to vote the restricted shares, even before being fully vested. Restricted stock also retains some value if the bank's stock price drops, unlike stock options, which become worthless if the stock price falls below the exercise price. Finally, dilution of current shareholders' ownership is usually less than for stock options, as fewer shares are sometimes granted under a restricted stock award.

Stock Appreciation Rights

Similar to stock options, stock appreciation rights ("SARs") enable an employee to share in the benefits of rising stock prices, but the holder is not required to pay a strike price to acquire the security. Instead, upon exercise, the holder receives the appreciation in value of the underlying stock. SARs often can be beneficial to banks with shareholder restrictions, such as S corporations, which limit the number of shareholders allowed to hold a company's stock. Additionally, the ownership dilution which accompanies option and restricted stock grants is not an issue with SARs, unless the appreciation is settled in shares rather than cash. Benefits to SARs holders are taxed upon exercise as ordinary income.

FINANCIAL ISSUES

There are differing opinions as to which type of equity incentive instrument is more beneficial to the issuing bank and recipient. The following discussion relates to various views of the incentives to employees, as well as potential tax and dilution implications for both the issuer and the holder. Given the complexity of these questions, we strongly urge you to get competent legal and tax advice before implementing any of the plans.

Incentives

Some compensation experts believe options encourage executives to inflate the stock price in the short run until their options can be exercised, reducing the focus on long-term goals. Restricted stock is by nature long-term (therefore reducing the possibility that executives will simply ride the bull market over a short period and cash out as soon as trouble hits) and has no expiration date. Additionally, the ability of restricted stock holders to receive dividends and vote their shares results in a closer alignment of executives' and shareholders' interests.

However, restricted stock retains some value even in the instance of a decline in stock price, and some opponents believe restricted stock is simply "pay-for-attendance," as executives are guaranteed a payout no matter what happens to the stock price. However, restricted stock awards can be structured so that they are tied to performance goals.

Tax Issues

As previously noted, ISO holders are typically taxed only upon the sale or transfer of their shares, while NQO holders are taxed at the exercise date. Restricted stock holders are not taxed at the time of grant, but rather, upon the vesting of the shares when the restrictions lapse. The fair market value of the shares (or the amount above what was paid for the stock, if applicable) at the time of vesting is subject to ordinary income tax rates. Additionally, the employee pays taxes on any dividends that he or she receives on the restricted stock. If the employee chooses, however, he or she may elect Section 83(b), which allows the holder to report income in the year the stock is granted, prior to vesting. When the stock is sold later, the holder reports a capital gain.

Employers may deduct only the holder's ISO compensation in the instance of a disqualifying disposition. Otherwise, the issuing bank receives no favorable tax treatment from issuing an ISO. In the case of NQOs, the employer receives a tax deduction equal to the amount of ordinary income recognized by the employee, as noted above. Employers also receive a similar deduction from the issuance of restricted stock.

IRC Section 409A originally became effective in January 2005, although the effective date was later extended to January 2008. Under Section 409A, options and stock appreciation rights awarded by companies must be valued at their fair market value on the date of grant. If options or SARs are issued with a strike price below their fair market value, the IRS believes they represent a form of deferred compensation, representing a shift of current compensation to a future taxable year. Previously, companies were allowed to establish option prices using "reasonable valuation methods." Following Section 409A, however, if the IRS finds that option strike prices are below fair market value (i.e., the options are "in the money" at the time of grant), the bank must prove that its original stock valuation was reasonable.

Dilution

Dilution may occur when additional shares are issued, either by direct sale, the conversion of convertible securities, or the exercise of options. Restricted stock awards immediately dilute existing shareholders' ownership percentages, as more shares are outstanding following the grant. Stock options may have a dilutive effect on the value of each share of stock outstanding. One way to assess the dilution is the "treasury stock method," which assumes that the granting bank uses the proceeds from the exercise of options to repurchase existing shares at the prevailing market price. Thus, the "fully diluted" total shares outstanding will increase by the number of options exercised, less the shares assumed to be repurchased by the bank with the option proceeds.

SECTION THREE

STOCK TRANSACTIONS

Money is not real. It is a conscious agreement on measuring value.

John Ralston Saul
Author

This section focuses on stock transactions and provides an overview of different types of stock transactions as well as the financial issues associated with each. Chapter 6 gives a summary of important issues to consider when a transfer of shares, either through an estate (after death) or through gifting (prior to death), occurs. Chapter 7 sheds some light on the financial considerations present when evaluating a number of different capital raising alternatives, including common stock, preferred stock, trust preferred securities, and subordinated debt. Chapter 7 also provides assistance if your bank is in the position to raise capital to support the asset base or, alternatively, has an opportunity to make an investment in another bank facing a capital shortfall. This is an important topic as the alternative ways to raise capital have substantially different impacts on existing shareholders and the bank's future returns. Chapter 8 provides a guide to understanding buy-sell agreements, specifically when one might be needed and how one might be constructed. Additionally, Chapter 8 briefly touches on specific financial issues with buy-sell agreements that can serve as recurring sources of difficulty.

CHAPTER 6

ESTATE & GIFT TAX ISSUES

In the typical private company, shares are often transferred from generation to generation. This commonly occurs in two ways: through an estate (after death) or gifting (prior to death). This chapter provides a brief introduction to important issues to consider when either type of transaction occurs.

Disclaimer: Mercer Capital does not offer tax or legal advice. We recommend consulting legal counsel and/or an accountant before taking any actions that have tax and/or legal ramifications. However, we have seen thousands of appraisals for gift and estate tax purposes so we are somewhat familiar with the subject.

OVERVIEW

One question that often arises from the need to report the value of private shares to taxing authorities is, "Will they want to see an appraisal?" The short answer is, "yes." A rough estimate of value, particularly when large sums of money are at stake, generally will not suffice. Revenue Ruling 59-60, which governs valuations performed for estate and gift tax purposes, specifically takes a position against formula appraisals and emphasizes rendering a value in the context of common sense, informed judgment, and reasonableness. Additionally, the appraiser should be independent of the parties involved.

FINANCIAL ISSUES

Estate Taxes

As an effort to make the lives of everyone involved easier, the first thing to think about once the estate's wheels have been set in motion is the tax filing deadline. Far too often, clients wait until weeks, if not days, before the estate tax filing deadline. The law allows nine months from the date of death before the tax forms must be filed; however, an extension is possible if the estate's tax liability is paid at the first due date. Getting an estate in order is certainly no easy task, but if the appraiser is given sufficient time to render the opinion, he or she is less likely to overlook anything or make a mistake.

Another benefit to starting earlier rather than later is that the appraiser has sufficient time to examine the value of the business at both possible valuation dates. Tax law provides that returns may be filed using the value of the shares at the date of death or the value at the "alternate date," which is six months following the date of death. If the industry or the market takes a turn for the worse shortly after the date of death or the bank has a rough six months, the value of the shares could be less at the alternate date. This could serve to decrease the estate tax burden.

Gift Taxes

One way to avoid a large estate tax burden is to gift shares in smaller increments over time. There are a number of advantages to transferring shares in this manner.

» **If the owning shareholder is relatively young (or has several decades over which to transfer ownership), the tax burden can be reduced significantly, or even eliminated.** The law allows annual gifts to an individual up to a specified limit (currently $12,000) without imposing any taxes. So, for example, if a shareholder has three children and five grandchildren to whom he would like to transfer a portion of ownership of the bank, he could transfer nearly $96,000 worth of stock annually without having to pay gift taxes. Over a number of years this can reduce the shareholder's position in the company significantly and, consequently, his or her associated estate tax burden. Typically, an appraisal is necessary at each gifting date.

» **The level of value at which the appraisal for gifting purposes is performed (see Chapter 2) is based on the size of the gift, not the size of the block of shares owned by the gifting shareholder.** In other words, although a shareholder may own 75% of the outstanding stock (generally considered a controlling interest), if that shareholder gifts 25% of the stock, the gift is considered a minority interest and marketability and minority discounts can apply. In essence, breaking a large block of stock into a number of smaller blocks to be gifted over a number of years can decrease tax liabilities for a controlling shareholder.

CHAPTER 7

RAISING CAPITAL

Banks raise capital to fund organic growth of the balance sheet, pursue acquisition strategies, and satisfy regulatory requirements. For regulatory purposes, capital is classified into two categories: Tier 1 and Tier 2. Tier 1 capital, or "core" capital, consists of shareholders' equity (both common stock and certain types of preferred stock), as well as a certain amount of trust preferred securities.[17] Tier 2 capital, or "supplementary" capital, consists of hybrid capital instruments not qualifying for Tier 1 treatment, subordinated debt, and some or all of the loan loss reserve. The alternatives for raising capital affect existing shareholders and the bank's future returns differently and are treated in different ways for regulatory capital purposes. The following discussion describes these instruments and their impacts on shareholders, earnings, and regulatory capital requirements.

COMMON STOCK

Overview

The most prevalent form of capital is common stock. It has the lowest liquidation preference of any capital instrument. A bank's total equity can be comprised of more than one class of common stock, with the various classes carrying different voting and dividend rights. However, only one class of common stock is allowed in order to qualify as a Subchapter S corporation. Issuing common stock places no pressure on the bank's cash flow if no dividends are declared; however, the primary disadvantage is the dilution that current shareholders may experience to their ownership positions and future earnings per share.

Issuing common stock is not always unfavorable from the perspective of existing shareholders. While all common stock issuances reduce (or "dilute") the ownership positions of the existing shareholders, not all issuances dilute the value of the existing shareholders' interest in the bank. For example, issuing stock to enable the bank to pursue a growth opportunity may enhance (or be "accretive" to) the value of the existing shareholders' shares of stock. Thus, from the perspective of shareholder value (the most important perspective from our standpoint), the issuance of common stock is beneficial. However, if the bank must issue common equity to replace equity that was lost through poor lending decisions, both the existing shareholders' ownership percentages and the value of their shares is typically diminished, as the new investors capture the upside from the bank's recovery (while perhaps necessary from the bank's perspective). A capital raise in these circumstances would most likely be an unfavorable event from the perspective of the existing shareholders.

Financial Issues

In considering a common stock issuance, important questions to consider include:

» **How should the transaction be structured?** Should the bank conduct a rights offering to existing shareholders? Should the bank sell stock to new investors who may bring additional expertise to the bank?

» **What perquisites of control, such as board seats, should the new investors be given?**

» **What share price balances the need to raise capital with the goal of minimizing or eliminating dilution to the existing shareholders?**

» **Should other incentives, such as warrants, be included in the "package" offered to investors?**

PREFERRED STOCK

Overview

An equity alternative to common stock is preferred stock, a separate class of equity that is senior to common stock and typically has no voting rights. In its simplest form, "straight" preferred stock simply pays the holder either a fixed or floating rate dividend. Convertible preferred stock is a hybrid instrument that combines elements of both straight preferred stock and common equity. Generally, convertible preferred stock has a lower dividend rate than straight preferred stock, but a higher dividend yield than common stock. To compensate investors for accepting the lower current return, the investors receive the right to participate in the appreciation of the common stock. Further, preferred stock dividends can be either cumulative (meaning that dividends are accrued with the intent of paying such dividends later) or non-cumulative (meaning that the preferred stock holder has no right to receive dividend payments missed by the bank).

Advantages of preferred stock include:

» Proceeds from the sale of preferred stock can generally be treated as Tier 1 capital, subject to certain limits. No formal limits exist on the amount of non-cumulative preferred stock a bank may include in Tier 1 capital, although certain informal limits exist on a bank's reliance on non-cumulative preferred stock. Cumulative preferred stock is includable in Tier 1 capital, subject to certain limits.

» For straight preferred stock, the bank can attract capital in a form that does not dilute the ownership of the existing common shareholders. Thus, the existing shareholders do not have to share any benefits related to future appreciation in the bank's stock price, unlike shareholders in a convertible preferred stock offering.

» For convertible preferred stock, a potentially lower dividend rate is possible relative to that obtainable by issuing straight preferred stock or subordinated debt.

Potential disadvantages include:

» The cash flow requirements to service the dividend payments.

» The absence of tax deductibility of the dividend payments.

From an investor's perspective, preferred stock can be an attractive alternative to common stock. For convertible preferred stock, the investor may receive a dividend in excess of the common stock's dividend, plus the right to enjoy appreciation in the underlying common stock. The higher dividend protects the investor's potential downside (to the extent the issuer actually pays the dividend). Further, if the investor is a corporation, a tax deduction for dividends received may be available.

Financial Issues

When structuring preferred stock, important considerations include:

» **What is the appropriate dividend rate?** This depends, in part, on the type of preferred stock (straight or convertible). In addition, the perceived credit quality of the issuer is of great importance. Typically, dividend rates on convertible preferred stocks are lower than those on straight issuances because of the conversion feature.

» **What is the appropriate conversion premium for convertible issues?** The conversion premium (at the date the preferred stock is issued) represents the extent to which the par value of the preferred stock exceeds the price of the common stock that would be received in the event of conversion. For example, consider one preferred share with a par value of $1,000 that can be converted into 20 common shares. The implied conversion price is $50 ($1,000 / 20 shares). If the value of the common stock on that date was also $50, the conversion premium is 0%. Generally, conversion premiums are greater than 0%, meaning that the common stock must appreciate before conversion becomes financially attractive. Issuing banks prefer higher conversion premiums, because fewer shares will be issued upon conversion. Continuing the preceding example, if the conversion premium is 20%, the conversion price would be $60 ($50 current common stock price x 1.20). Then, upon conversion, the bank would issue only 16.7

shares ($1,000 par value / $60 conversion price). Conversely, investors prefer lower conversion premiums.

» **Should the dividends be cumulative?** This issue affects the capital treatment of the proceeds as well as the potential return, and may be a matter of negotiations with potential investors.

» **Do the terms of the convertible stock meet applicable regulatory guidance for consideration in Tier 1 capital?** For instance, structures that create an incentive for the bank to redeem the preferred stock for cash, particularly in times of financial distress, may render the security ineligible for inclusion in capital.

TRUST PREFERRED SECURITIES

Overview

Trust preferred securities ("TPS") are a hybrid instrument, combining the tax treatment of debt and the Tier 1 capital treatment of equity. TPS are issued by first creating and issuing debt to a trust (a special purpose entity). The trust then issues trust preferred securities, which pay distributions at fixed or floating rates, to investors. Next, the trust purchases a subordinated debenture from the bank holding company using the proceeds from the sale of trust preferred securities. Because the interest paid on the debenture is tax-deductible, the bank may realize tax benefits and the trust preferred securities are generally includable in regulatory capital, subject to certain limits.

Initially, TPS were issued primarily by large banks in significant amounts through public offerings. Later, pooled offerings became more popular, which allowed several banks to share the costs of the offering and lowered the offering size for individual banks participating in the pool. This created the opportunity for smaller banks to issue TPS.

Financial Issues

The favorable after-tax cost of capital represents one of the primary advantages of issuing trust preferreds. Prior to late 2007, community banks could easily access the capital markets by participating in one of the pooled offerings underwritten by investment banks. As conditions in the credit markets deteriorated with the advent of the subprime mortgage crisis, this opportunity disappeared. Pooled offerings have vanished from the marketplace, although they may eventually return if investor demand improves. However, banks still can consider issuing trust preferred securities to local investors through private placements. Although this type of offering may require more time and professional fees than a pooled offering, the bank still enjoys the significant tax and capital benefits. Questions to consider regarding whether to issue trust preferred securities include:

» **If the bank issues securities to local investors, what is an appropriate rate?** Selecting a rate would depend upon, among other considerations, the structure of the offering (e.g., fixed versus floating rate payments), credit quality (e.g., the capital ratios and loan quality of the issuer), the interest rate environment, and market pricing of comparable instruments.

» **What are the capital implications?** While current capital rules permit a bank to include trust preferred securities in Tier 1 capital, these rules will eventually be tightened. Currently, the capital rules limit trust preferred securities includable as Tier 1 capital to 25% of core capital elements. Eventually, core capital elements will exclude goodwill, thus reducing the amount of trust preferred securities that qualify as capital for institutions with goodwill.

SUBORDINATED DEBT

Overview

In the event that the bank needs to raise Tier 2 capital, subordinated debentures may be desirable. Subordinated debentures may be included in Tier 2 capital, subject to a limitation that Tier 2 capital may not exceed 50% of Tier 1 capital. Like trust preferred securities, interest payments on subordinated debentures are tax deductible. Subordinated debentures can be issued at the subsidiary bank level, which may decrease their credit risk for investors, relative to instruments that require the holding company to maintain sufficient liquidity from bank dividends or other sources of funds.

Financial Issues

For community banks where subordinated debentures may be utilized, the following questions should be considered.

» **What is the interest rate?** Similar to setting the interest rate on trust preferred securities, an analysis should consider market interest rates, rates on similar subordinated debentures, and the credit quality of the issuer.

» **What is the capital treatment?** Subordinated debentures have various capital limits and phase-outs. Over the five years prior to the debenture's maturity, the amount includable in Tier 2 capital declines by 20% per year. In addition, the amount of subordinated debentures includable in Tier 2 capital is limited to 50% of Tier 1 capital. To the extent that new capital guidelines limit the amount of trust preferred securities includable in Tier 1 capital, a bank may find a portion of its trust preferred securities included in Tier 2 capital. In that case, the trust preferred securities and subordinated debentures would collectively be subject to the 50% limit.

The following chart summarizes the advantages and disadvantages of the instruments discussed in this chapter.

Common Stock	
Issuer Perspective	**Investor Perspective**
Advantages	**Advantages**
Favored from a regulatory standpoint	Potentially greater returns than holding straight preferred stock or debt
No cash flow issues unless dividends paid	For significant investments, ability to provide greater input (such as through board seats)
Disadvantages	**Disadvantages**
Dilution to existing shareholders	Greater downside risk than instruments like preferred stock with better yields
May have to offer board seats or other perquisites of control	Potentially no cash flow, if no dividends paid by bank
	Potential future dilution in the event additional capital is required
	Potential illiquidity

Preferred Stock	
Issuer Perspective	**Investor Perspective**
Advantages	**Advantages**
Less dilutive than a common stock offering	Downside protection vis-a-vis common stock from dividend
A straight preferred offering is non-dilutive to common shareholders	Share upside with common stock in convertible offerings
In a convertible offering, issuer may obtain a lower dividend rate than straight preferred	Dividends receive deduction
Includable in Tier 1 capital, subject to certain limits	
Disadvantages	**Disadvantages**
Dividend payments are not tax deductible	Dividend could be eliminated, and payments may not be cumulative
Informal limits exist on the amount of non-cumulative preferred stock includable in Tier 1 capital	May not have voting rights, unlike common stock
Formal limits exist on the amount of cumulative preferred stock included in Tier 1 capital	
Shareholder dilution in convertible offerings	

Trust Preferred Securites	
Issuer Perspective	**Investor Perspective**
Advantages	**Advantages**
No shareholder dilution	Spreads to LIBOR widened in late 2007 and 2008
Favorable tax treatment	
Includable in Tier 1 capital, subject to certain limits	
Historically the lowest cost form of Tier 1 capital	
Disadvantages	**Disadvantages**
Difficulty in accessing the market in current environment	Distributions can be deferred, generally for 20 quarters
Spreads to LIBOR have widened	Holder is deeply subordinate in overall capital structure
Limits exist on the amount includable in Tier 1 capital. These limits will eventually tighten	Generally no ability to participate in appreciation of common stock

Subordinated Debentures	
Issuer Perspective	**Investor Perspective**
Advantages	**Advantages**
Provides Tier 2 capital	May offer greater assurance of receiving payments than other instruments, if issued at bank level
Interest payments are tax deductible	
Generally no shareholder dilution	
Disadvantages	**Disadvantages**
Does not help with Tier 1 capital shortfall	Generally no ability to participate in appreciation of common stock
Phase-out of amount includable in Tier 2 capital	

CHAPTER 8

BUY-SELL AGREEMENTS[18]

Buy-sell agreements are generally created by and among the shareholders of a company and the company itself. They also may be between businesses in the form of joint venture agreements. The mechanism of the buy-sell agreement can be in the form of a separate document, or embedded in the operating agreement or another corporate document. Among other things, a buy-sell agreement serves to establish the price at which certain future transactions will take place upon the occurrence of a "trigger event." Make sure any buy-sell agreement is clear, concise, and well-constructed from a legal and valuation perspective.

OVERVIEW

The valuation provisions of buy-sell agreements are implemented upon the occurrence of a trigger event. Common types of trigger events occur when a shareholder who is employed by the company quits, dies, is fired, retires, or is disabled. All of these trigger events have two things in common: 1) in each of them, a shareholder who works for the bank ceases to do so for one reason or another, and 2) they are all unpleasant to think about. In fact, management and boards of directors often ignore the need for a buy-sell agreement simply because the subjects that must be addressed in the planning process are just too sensitive.

There also can be events other than those listed above that might require the need to repurchase an employee's shares. For example, an employee going through a divorce may be forced by the courts to liquidate all or some of his or her stock in the bank. This trigger event also presents the possibility that the non-employee spouse may gain a portion (even a controlling interest) of the bank's stock absent an agreement that prevents that from happening. (For more information regarding the divorce of a key shareholder and the possible implications of such an event, see Chapter 18.)

Lastly, buy-sell agreements are a common means for banks that have elected S corporation status to preserve the S election. A proposed transfer of shares by an existing shareholder to a non-shareholder often gives the other existing shareholders or the bank (holding company) the right to purchase those shares.

How Buy-Sell Agreements Are Constructed

Generally, buy-sell agreements are constructed by attorneys. Often, the attorney has a template from which the buy-sell agreement is created. While specific items may vary from company to company, these agreements typically have generic features and language.

Following are the four general types of buy-sell agreements.

» **Fixed Price Agreements** fix the price of future purchases at a specific dollar amount by stating a value for the equity of the enterprise, either in dollars or as a per-share value.

» **Formula Agreements** establish the price by providing a formula for determining value. Examples include a multiple of book value or earnings. The agreement also may call for an averaging of valuation indications developed using two or more formulas.

» **Shotgun Agreements** outline a process whereby one party offers to purchase (or sell) shares and the other party has the right or the obligation to sell (or purchase) the shares at the offered price.

» **Process Agreements** outline a process by which future transactions will be priced. In nearly all cases, process agreements call upon the use of one or more business appraisers in the process of determining the price.

While each type of agreement has advantages and disadvantages, we encourage the use of process agreements. Notwithstanding the obvious bias of an appraisal firm promoting an agreement that requires its services, process agreements more often than not have the highest likelihood of determining a price that is most appropriate to both buyers and sellers at the relevant date. However, process agreements are not without their pitfalls. You must define the valuation assignment accurately (as described previously in Chapter 1) in terms that are widely accepted within the business valuation community. For this task, having a business appraiser serve as a consultant to aid in the preparation of an agreement, or at least to review the agreement before it is finalized, is often helpful. Once the agreement becomes final, anything that is unclear could cost substantial time and money to resolve.

FINANCIAL ISSUES

As noted above, there are numerous issues to consider when structuring a buy-sell agreement. However, a few items seem to be recurring sources of difficulty.

Funding with Life Insurance

Life insurance is one option for funding a buy-sell agreement. Other options include cash (either cash already held at the holding company or upstreamed from the banking subsidiary as needed) or new borrowings.

In the case of funding the agreement with life insurance, the agreement must specify how the life insurance proceeds are to be treated in the valuation to determine the purchase price. There are two broad options here: 1) include the life insurance proceeds in the calculation of value, or 2) do not include them. Clearly, the inclusion of the proceeds leads to a higher (sometimes significantly higher) purchase price for the shares, which is usually a good thing for the seller and a bad thing for the buyer. The easiest way for appraisers to determine how to treat the proceeds is for the buy-sell agreement to define treatment of life insurance explicitly. Absent these instructions, the appraiser has to use his or her own best judgment about how to treat the proceeds, and one side will likely be disappointed.

Level of Value

The most critical point to make here is not that one level of value is more appropriate than another, but that both parties agree to and clearly specify which level of value will be used (for more discussion on levels of value, see Chapter 2). If the company has a process agreement that calls for two appraisers, and one appraiser assumes a control level of value while the other assumes a nonmarketable minority level of value, then the odds are high that the two appraisers will reach significantly different conclusions. Even if only one appraiser is involved, if one side is under the impression that the agreement calls for a certain level of value and the other side is under a different impression entirely, then someone is going to be surprised by the concluded value. Surprises in these situations can lead to hard feelings, discontent, and even legal disputes.

S Corporation

Having a plan regarding the transfer of ownership is particularly important in cases where the bank is an S corporation. Given the restrictions on the number and types of shareholders allowed in S corporations, an unforeseen event, such as a shareholder's death, may jeopardize the S corporation status. If a shareholder were to die, absent a buy-sell agreement and the planning involved in developing such an agreement, the shareholder's estate might distribute the shares to either a) non-qualifying shareholders, or b) several shareholders that might then push the total number of shareholders above the maximum permissible level.

Determining Who Bears the Cost

Process agreements that call for an appraisal (and sometimes several appraisals) can become costly. At the outset, the bank and the shareholders should determine which party will be responsible for the cost. While there is no hard and fast rule about how the process should be funded, here are some things to keep in mind.

» The bank can pay for the expense in pre-tax dollars.

» The remaining shareholders experience a pro rata increase in percentage ownership following the transaction. The selling shareholder receives no such benefit.

» The bank is likely more able to afford an experienced, well-qualified appraiser than the selling shareholder, creating a potential disadvantage at the outset.

» Knowing the value of the bank stock is an ancillary benefit to management.

» Charging the selling shareholder "transaction costs," similar to those that would be incurred upon the sale of the bank, is another option.

CONCLUSION

While this chapter merely scratches the surface regarding the construction of a buy-sell agreement, our purpose is to illustrate the importance of such agreements; not only the importance of creating them, but the importance of constructing them properly. Buy-sell agreements are complex legal and business documents that can have a profound impact on the bank and its future shareholders long after the agreement has been triggered and the transaction has occurred. The bottom line: Anything not written in the agreement has not been decided upon or agreed to. In buy-sell agreements, more is better.

SECTION FOUR

STRATEGIC ALTERNATIVES

> My job is to listen to ideas, maybe cook up a few of my own, and make decisions based on what's good for the shareholders and for the company.
>
> Philip Knight
> *Chairman, Nike, Inc.*

This section focuses on a number of strategic alternatives that may serve to increase shareholder value. Chapter 9 provides a list of important questions to consider before buying another bank or selling your own bank, and gives a brief overview of the transaction process from initial planning to closing. Chapter 10 provides additional information on the final aspect of the merger/sale process; the fairness opinion. Chapter 10 also answers a number of questions that we are frequently asked by boards regarding fairness opinions. Chapter 11 focuses specifically on capital gains and dividends. Chapter 12 focuses on Subchapter S conversions and provides an overview of the basic differences between an S corporation and a C corporation, including the advantages and disadvantages of each. Additionally, Chapter 12 summarizes the process for making an S election and gives a brief look at how this S election might affect the valuation of your institution.

CHAPTER 9

MERGERS & ACQUISITIONS

This chapter provides an overview of the transaction process, as well as significant issues to discuss when considering a merger or acquisition. The decision to buy or sell a bank is among the most important decisions ever made by management and the board of directors. The question of independent ownership versus consolidation with another banking organization should be resolved through a comprehensive strategic business planning process. A number of factors are important in reaching this decision. A full discussion of these elements is outside the scope of this book, however, some of the most important factors are the bank's marketplace, financial and managerial strength, products and services, operating efficiency, capital requirements, growth potential, and the desires of the shareholders regarding liquidity.

OVERVIEW

If your bank is committed to selling, a number of steps must be completed prior to the closing of the transaction. Typically, the merger and acquisition process can be split into three phases: planning, materials preparation/ marketing, and negotiations and due diligence/closing. The following outline includes those steps to be completed by the transaction advisor, who is retained to assist with the selling of the bank. We have found that those banks who retain a transaction advisor receive more favorable pricing and terms than those who do not. A number of other important steps handled by other advisors, such as completing regulatory applications, are not included in the following transaction outline.

Phase I – Planning

Important steps of the planning phase include:

- **Collection of information on the bank**, including historical financial statements, budgets, and multi-year projections.
- **On-site due diligence visit** with management as needed.
- **Preparation of an analysis of strategic alternatives available to the bank**, which provides an overview of options available to the bank's board of directors. This type of analysis typically includes the following:
    - The history of the enterprise from inception.
    - The economic outlook in general for the markets served by the bank.
    - The financial condition of the bank, including the bank's earning capacity.
    - Potential synergies to be realized from the perspective of one or more strategic buyers.
    - The bank's performance relative to a peer group of comparable banks.
    - Specific analysis of the individual potential strategic alternatives, such as remaining independent, declaring a special dividend, or engaging in a sale of the bank to a third party, including consideration of the strengths and weaknesses of each alternative.

Phase II – Materials Preparation and Marketing

Important steps of the materials preparation and marketing phase include:

- **Preparation of a Confidential Descriptive Memorandum**, which typically includes historical financial statements (Call Reports, Y-9s, audits, etc.) and other background information. The Confidential Descriptive Memorandum is intended to provide the interested parties with insight into the bank, while at the same time maintaining the confidentiality of proprietary information about the business, to the extent possible.

» **Development of a list of potential acquirers** based upon a review of banks located in the region, supplemented with management's insight into who the more likely candidates may be.

» **Conducting the marketing process** through contacting potential acquirers, on a selected basis, who will be asked to execute confidentiality agreements before receiving the Confidential Descriptive Memorandum.

» **Delivery of a copy of the Confidential Descriptive Memorandum** to the parties, on a selected basis, which have expressed an interest in the bank.

» **Request a best indication of value by a specific date**. The parties will be expected to address price, proposed terms, etc.

» **Review of the expressions of interest** (or letters of intent) received from the contacted parties to determine which offer(s) provide the best price and terms in which a transaction can be consummated.

Phase III – Negotiation and Due Diligence / Closing

Important steps of the negotiation and due diligence/closing phase include:

» **Negotiations with the prospective party(ies)** in order to reach a business transaction for the acquisition of the bank.

» **Assistance in facilitating the buyer's due diligence**.

» **Support of the legal document drafting process** to make sure that the legal documents reflect the business transaction from a financial point of view.

» **If appropriate, preparation of the fairness opinion** (discussed fully in Chapter 10), Fairness Memorandum, and other appropriate documents in order to consummate the transaction.

» **Closing**.

FINANCIAL ISSUES

A list of questions is provided to highlight a number of financial issues to consider before buying another bank or selling your own bank. We find these questions to be beneficial for clients when contemplating a transaction.

Questions to Consider Before Buying

» **What is your bank's motivation for acquiring?** There should be a number of compelling reasons for acquiring another bank. Common factors motivating buyers include diversification into new markets or other lines of business, improved economies of scale, potential to improve the acquired bank's profitability, expansion into a higher growth market, acquiring management depth, and so on.

» **Who is the acquisition target(s)?** Generally, the answer to this question is driven by your bank's response to the first question, and those banks that provide the factors you are seeking should be targeted. For example, if you are interested in diversifying into new markets and product lines, then approach banks which meet those criteria.

» **When should your bank consider making an acquisition?** Acquiring another institution can take a considerable amount of time and energy, which can distract management from running the underlying business. Thus, you should engage in a transaction when management has the capacity to focus on it. Distraction of management is an opportunity cost that can negatively impact near-term operating results of the existing bank. Experience tells us that distraction generally is underestimated by management.

» **How is your bank going to engage in this acquisition effort?** As noted previously, conducting an acquisition takes a great deal of time and energy. Thus, a plan that outlines the M&A process should be considered and appropriate external advisors (legal, accounting, and financial) contacted so that the process runs smoothly and the deal can be accomplished within a reasonable timeframe.

» **How is your bank's timing?** Bankers often use rules of thumb (such as some multiple of book value) in considering M&A opportunities. However, the valuation of bank acquisitions is more variable than suggested by these rules of thumb; thus, directors should be aware of the current bank M&A market prior to launching an acquisition strategy. Relatively high bank acquisition prices may suggest other questions, such as: Are we buying at the peak of the market? Should we keep some "dry powder" and wait for a more opportune environment? Can we minimize some of the risk of acquiring in a "hot" market by offering our own stock as consideration, rather than cash?

» **How is your bank going to integrate the acquisition?** Your bank must begin planning for the integration of the acquired institution prior to engaging in the M&A process. The acquirer should be able to see how the target would fit into their business plan and objectives. Keep in mind that the end objective is not to acquire an institution but to run one profitable institution after successfully integrating the acquired institution. Beginning the process with the ultimate objective – a successfully integrated, profitable institution – in mind is important.

Questions to Consider Before Selling

» **What is your bank's motivation for selling?** There should be a number of compelling factors. Common factors include relatively favorable acquisition pricing, relatively strong earnings performance, a challenging operating environment, the increased burden of regulatory costs, or an aging management or ownership group.

» **How is your bank's timing?** Since you only have one chance to sell the bank, timing is of crucial importance. Banks are often faced with the sell-now versus sell-later question in trying to maximize shareholder value. Resolving this issue requires assessment of the M&A environment. By selling, the bank may be able to command a premium, because buying may be cheaper than building for the acquirer. Also, the bank avoids the potentially diminished profits that may occur if the bank does not sell and new competitors enter the market.

» **Is selling the institution the best strategic alternative to achieve your bank's objective?** We have generally found that the best time to sell a business is when the industry is "hot" (which refers to an industry with a relatively large number of deals and high pricing multiples), and/or the company's recent performance is "hot" (with recent strong earnings performance). If the timing is not right, transaction advisors can be utilized to explore strategic alternatives, such as remaining independent or declaring a special dividend.

» **Should a financial advisor be retained?** We conducted a study in 2007 that found empirical evidence supporting the retention of a transaction advisor when selling your bank.[19] In this study, the pricing multiples received by those banks who retained a transaction advisor were compared to those who did not. Our analysis revealed that those banks sold with the assistance of a transaction advisor received a 20% higher price to earnings multiple and a 15% higher price to tangible book multiple, which more than offset the estimated costs of hiring the transaction advisor. Consequently, a seasoned financial advisor should generally be retained to both facilitate the exploration of a number of strategic alternatives (in addition to an outright sale) available to the bank and hopefully increase the economic proceeds to the sellers. Additionally, an advisor eliminates the potential distraction for management and the board from taking the 'For Sale by Owner" approach.

» **Is your bank ready for sale?** Experienced acquirers often add 10% to 25% to the bottom line in the first year or two of ownership by achieving income and expense improvements. The bank's owners may enhance the franchise's value by improving operating performance prior to sale or engaging a transaction advisor who can create a sound argument to the buyer for any profit enhancement the buyer can expect to capture and demand that the client be paid for it.

» **Are there any special considerations that your bank wants to receive in the deal?** Business owners have unique objectives to consider when selling their business. The seller should make clear to its advisor any concessions that it desires (such as the retention of current employees at their current salary levels, to the extent feasible) prior to engaging in the process.

Merger of Equals

Another strategic alternative that banks often consider is a merger of equals ("MOE") transaction. Following are some common questions.

» **What is a merger of equals?** A merger of equals is a merger of banks of roughly the same size. Typically, assets of one bank will fall between 67% and 133% of the other. The interests of the respective parties are advanced by a mutual continuation of their businesses, and often no, or a very low, premium is paid by one institution to the other.

» **What are some advantages/disadvantages of a MOE?** Banks of similar size often merge to collectively enhance their market share and presence, and avoid being swallowed up by much larger competitors. Newer markets can be explored and certain growth barriers become obsolete. Often, the consolidation of institutions provides opportunities to enhance earnings and value due to the economies of scale that result from the combination.

  However, a MOE may not always be advantageous. If consolidated properly, a MOE can resolve many management issues; yet conflict can arise. The two merging institutions must have a strategic plan that covers the combined banks' upper level management, board of directors, etc. If not, this can lead to internal strife with the merged institution.

» **What are the steps to initiating a MOE?** First, an institution must identify potential partners in the same or nearby markets. The institution must then decide if the deal would add value to the existing institution. In-depth research should be done on each potential institution to identify opportunities for synergies.

  Once a contact and a relationship have been made, the institution must sell the concept and its ideas and values to the other. Ideas of mutual benefit and cohesion must be reiterated to establish a feeling of trust among the two institutions.

» **What are some other important questions to ask when considering a MOE?** A MOE is often a difficult transaction to perform because both institutions will have to answer questions such as:

  - Who becomes president, CEO, CFO of the emerging company?
  - Who will retain seats on the board of directors?
  - What will be the name of the consolidated institution?
  - Where will the headquarters be?

These are just a few of the many questions that must be answered in order for the bank resulting from a MOE to succeed.

CHAPTER 10

FAIRNESS OPINIONS

The following discussion relates to fairness opinions, which are the final aspect of the merger/sale process. A fairness opinion is an opinion, usually prepared in a brief letter, in which an independent financial advisor (typically an investment banking firm, valuation firm, or a specialized firm with appropriate credentials) renders an opinion that a proposed transaction is fair, from a financial point of view, to the shareholders (or a special group of shareholders) of a company.

OVERVIEW

The fairness opinion involves a review of the transaction from a financial point of view, including price, terms, and consideration received. Fairness opinions are viewed by many as recognition that the board of directors acted in good faith and in the interest of all shareholders (or the relevant class of stakeholders).

Typically, the fairness opinion is issued to a company's full board of directors or to special, independent committees of the board, and is issued on behalf of all shareholders or a specific group of shareholders. It is designed to assist directors in making reasonable business decisions and to provide protection under the "business judgment rule." The business judgment rule generally requires the following: a business decision is made; the board *exercised due care* in the process of making that decision; the board in this case *acted independently and objectively* (as a disinterested party might have acted); the board's decision was made in *good faith*; and there was *no abuse of discretion* in making the decision (*emphasis added*).

In the landmark case, *Smith v. Van Gorkom,* [488 A.2d 858 (Supreme Court of Delaware, 1985)], the Delaware Supreme Court effectively expanded the business judgment rule to encompass a requirement for informed decisions. Some important business lessons from the Court's decision include:

» The presence of a merger premium alone, as compared to the market price of the selling company, was not a sufficient reason to approve the merger, and directors were obligated to seek other sound valuation advice.

» The board made efforts believed to have a curative effect on any shortcomings, including hiring an investment banker to seek competitive bids and attaining the overwhelming support of the majority of shareholders.

» The Delaware court ruled that negligence occurred because the procedures for reaching the decisions were inadequate.

» The directors were held personally liable for a multi-million dollar judgment (beyond insurance coverage) for breach of their fiduciary duty.

In summary, the lessons of *Smith v. Van Gorkom* should cause directors to insist that significant transactions are presented to competent experts who can speak to the legal, valuation, and disclosure issues. The application of the Court's findings is a matter of legal judgment and expert legal counsel should be sought to assure that a board involved in a merger is complying fully with state and federal statutes and related court decisions.

When Are Fairness Opinions Required or Desired?

There are no specific guidelines regarding when to obtain a fairness opinion. Although not all-inclusive, managers and directors should consider obtaining a fairness opinion if one or more of the following situations are present.

» When the facts of particular transactions can lead reasonable (or unreasonable) stakeholders (or their friends, families, or advisors) to believe that other, preferable alternatives exist.

» When there is risk of misunderstandings about a deal or the potential for litigation that can kill transactions or spoil their aftermath.

» When a bank has several or many shareholders outside the immediate control group (which may be the board), or when the shareholder base is large and diverse.

» When there is the reality or perception that insiders could take advantage of their positions to enrich themselves.

Additionally, a fairness opinion should be obtained in merger or sale transactions when:

» Competing bids are received that are different in price or structure, thereby requiring an interpretation and comparison of the offers.

» The bank's recent financial performance prior to the transaction was poor.

» An offer is hostile or unsolicited.

» Directors lack unanimity over the appropriateness of selling at the present time, the adequacy of the offer(s), or both.

» A concern that some stakeholders might not fully understand or appreciate the degree of effort the board expended to assure adequacy of consideration and fairness to all stakeholders.

» The board is offered consideration involving shares, preferred shares, debt, or other securities in another public or private company that requires independent investigation.

» There are different classes of stakeholders, and there is or could appear to be a differential treatment of the classes.

» Competing bids were not solicited (i.e., the bank intentionally limited negotiations to one party only).

» Additional information about the acquiring bank is desired, particularly in a stock-for-stock transaction.

Lastly, a fairness opinion is often needed in non-merger circumstances when:

» Significant stock repurchase programs are planned for private or quasi-public companies.

» Affiliated parties are involved in the transaction.

The Role of the Financial Advisor

The financial advisor has a number of roles in constructing the fairness opinion, but the following list generally describes the primary ones.

» Determine the nature and the value of the securities or ownership interests to be given up (or the reasonable range of value) in exchange for the securities or consideration to be received, which also must be valued (within a reasonable range) and their nature (e.g., degree of marketability) examined.

» Know the standard of value for purposes of the transaction (see Chapter 2); however, that determination ultimately may involve a legal opinion from counsel or a court.

» Evaluate the financial terms and conditions of the proposed transaction (and compare with terms and conditions of other deals when feasible).

» Perform appropriate investigation of the terms of the transaction.

» Examine the documentation relating to the deal (letter of intent, definitive agreement, shareholder proxy statements, etc.) from a financial perspective.

» Advise the board of directors (or the special committee of the board of directors) of issues, concerns, or problems with a proposed deal from a financial point of view.

» Finally, opine as to the fairness, from a financial point of view, of the proposed transaction from the standpoint of a specific group of shareholders (e.g., all the shareholders, the minority shareholders, the holders of a particular class of securities, etc.).

FINRA Rule 2290 and the Implications for Banks

In October 2007, the SEC approved a new rule regarding fairness opinions called Financial Institutions Regulatory Authority ("FINRA") Rule 2290. While Rule 2290 is applicable only to member firms of FINRA, it is likely to become a best practices standard by which all fairness opinions are evaluated. In essence, Rule 2290 outlines disclosure guidelines to ensure quality control in the preparation of a fairness opinion. The rule is divided into six main parts, and each part largely relates to required disclosures of the firm issuing the fairness opinion (i.e., a valuation, investment banking, or other financial advisory firm), referred to in the following as the "issuing firm."

» **Contingent Compensation.** The issuing firm must disclose any contingent compensation, or any significant payment, that is to be received upon completion of the transaction.

» **Preceding Relationships.** Shareholders must be informed of any relationships within the past two years between the firm issuing the fairness opinion and the party hiring the issuing firm. However, the hiring firm can be confident that no sensitive information will be divulged, as the disclosure is meant only to be descriptive, not quantitative.

» **Independent Verification of Information.** The issuing firm must disclose whether or not any underlying information was verified independently.

» **Approval by a Fairness Committee.** The issuing firm must disclose whether or not the opinion was approved by a fairness committee within the issuing firm.

» **Fairness of Compensation.** The issuing firm must disclose whether or not an opinion about the fairness of compensation to company officers, directors, or employees is expressed.

» **Written Procedures.** The issuing firm must develop written procedures describing the types of transactions and circumstances in which a fairness committee is used. These procedures must include the process for committee personnel selection, qualifications of committee personnel, and the promotion of a balanced review of the opinion.

Several conclusions applicable to banks can be drawn from the FINRA rule. FINRA is attempting to provide shareholders with more information and allow them to make their own decisions regarding the existence of conflicts. However, the various parties to the transaction and their advisors still appear to be responsible for ensuring that no conflicts exist, or at the very least, that conflicts are minimized. Despite the new disclosure rules, any time the advisor on a deal prepares the fairness opinion or any time compensation for preparation of the fairness opinion is on a contingent basis, there exists the possibility for real or perceived conflicts of interest.

Further, FINRA pays significant attention to quality control issues within the firm issuing the fairness opinion. While some of these issues would be rendered moot if FINRA simply would disallow firms with potentially large conflicts of interest from preparing the fairness opinion, the focus does indeed center on what is in the best interest of the shareholder.

Second Fairness Opinions

Many investment banking firms that are hired to complete a transaction are frequently retained to provide a fairness opinion on the same transaction. This creates an obvious conflict of interest if the investment banking firm has a financial interest in the transaction or an existing relationship with the company or other parties involved in the transaction. Boards often would be well-advised to retain a truly independent firm to issue a second fairness opinion in such case (particularly in light of FINRA Rule 2290).

FINANCIAL ISSUES

While the fairness opinion itself is typically a short document, the supporting work behind the fairness opinion letter is considerable. The completion of analytical work is critical to the development of the fairness opinion. A fairness opinion should be based upon a number of considerations, including a review of at least the following five factors.

1. Financial performance and factors affecting earnings for the buyer, target, and the combined company.

2. Dividend paying history and capacity of the target and the combined company.

3. Pricing of transactions involving comparable financial institutions (i.e., comparable in such factors as geographic location, asset size, and profitability).

4. The investment characteristics of the acquiring bank if stock is received (including growth prospects and future profitability before and after the transaction).

5. The merger agreement and its terms.

Factor 3 noted above may also require the financial advisor to perform a valuation of the subject bank. Depending on the circumstances, the financial advisor may perform a number of analyses including a sell-now versus sell-later analysis, an analysis of comparable transactions, and/or a comparison to comparable publicly traded banks.

In addition to these five factors, the consideration of a number of other elements of the transaction may be necessary. A review of the process of the proposed transaction is often critical to evaluating the transaction. Important questions to consider in the review of the process include: Did the Board make an intentional decision to engage in a transaction, or is the company's involvement the result of a reaction to initiative(s) from outside? Who initiated the transaction? Was there any preliminary analysis of pricing or shareholder options prior to the initiation of the transaction process? What type of process was undertaken (i.e., negotiated sale, limited auction, or full auction)?

When reviewing alternative transactions, directors, managers, and their financial advisor should note that not all offers are directly comparable. Other factors to consider when evaluating pricing include the type of consideration paid (i.e., all stock, a consideration of both stock and cash, or all cash) and the terms of the transaction. Additionally, an examination of the value of the subject transaction to the seller's shareholders should be performed in certain situations. For example, items like contingent consideration (such as earn-outs) and escrow arrangements need to be evaluated and their contribution to the overall deal value estimated.

Are Some Deals More Fair than Others?

One important item to remember regarding a fairness opinion is that it is a range concept. Deals are negotiated based upon relative strengths and desires of the negotiators. There may be a range of outcomes at which a deal can be "fair," and, indeed, some deals are "more fair" than others. Fairness is judged from the viewpoint of one side only (the other side has to concern itself with fairness from its viewpoint).

Does a Fairness Opinion Guarantee that the Bank Received the Best Possible Deal?

No, a fairness opinion is no guarantee for a board of directors or a company's shareholders that the proposed deal is the best possible deal.

CHAPTER 11

CAPITAL GAINS & DIVIDENDS

Shareholder returns generally come in two forms: capital gains and dividends. This chapter begins by summarizing certain methods for generating capital gains from the disposition of shares and then goes on to focus on a few important items for banks to consider when establishing their dividend policy.

OVERVIEW

Capital Gains

A desire for access to liquidity is prevalent among shareholders of all companies. Liquidity for a minority interest is present in an investment when that interest (e.g. shares in a financial institution) can be converted into cash during a reasonable time period without loss of value. The majority of privately held community banks have relatively small shareholder bases and limited transaction volume, which results in limited liquidity. While privately held banks are generally more liquid than the typical closely held business, the limited marketability of minority interests in community bank stocks can be a problem.

In Chapter 9, we discussed the prospect of selling the institution, which represents one option for providing liquidity and generating a return for shareholders. Below, we outline some other commonly used strategies for providing liquidity in the shares of a community bank.

» **Stock Repurchase Plans.** While banks generally are prohibited from engaging in transactions in their own stock, bank holding companies do not operate under this regulatory restriction. A number of bank holding companies have regular share repurchase programs, while others engage in such programs infrequently, if ever.

» **Employee Stock Ownership Plans.** As discussed in Chapter 4, an ESOP can be used to help make a market in the shares and provide an increased level of liquidity for shareholders.

» **Efforts to Increase Market Activity.** Some community banks try to establish relationships with local brokers or with the local offices of national brokerage operations to encourage them to make a market in their shares. One disadvantage of this approach is that these efforts rarely increase the liquidity for a bank's shares, and, in most cases, the brokers only match buyers and sellers rather than taking the positions necessary to develop markets. Other efforts to increase market activity include the bank's officers attempting to match buyers and sellers of the institution's shares.

If bank management is unable to create liquidity for the shareholders, then the pressure to sell the bank may increase, particularly for those banks with aging and multi-generational shareholder bases. Further, if the financial performance of the bank slips, the pressure for liquidity may increase, and shareholders may try to achieve financial diversification by selling their interest now rather than awaiting the results of a turnaround of indefinite duration.

Dividends

Earnings are a primary source of bank capital. More precisely stated, retained earnings (net income less dividends paid to shareholders) are the primary capital source. Directors and management need to use caution in establishing a dividend policy because such policies can impact share values.

» **What is the normal dividend payout ratio for a bank?** Historically, publicly traded banks (that are C corporations) have paid approximately 30-35% of their earnings (net income) in shareholder dividends.

» **When should a bank pay a lower-than-average dividend?** Banks able to generate an above-average return on equity and also having reinvestment and growth opportunities can typically justify a below-average dividend payout ratio, in the range of 0% - 25%.

» **When should a bank pay a higher-than-average dividend?** Banks with a below-normal return on equity and below-normal growth opportunities should consider raising dividends to the higher end of the normal range. By doing so, the bank rewards shareholders with current income and avoids the accumulation of excess (underperforming) equity.

» **What is a special dividend policy and when should it be used?** A policy of special dividends consists of issuing a fairly low regular dividend, perhaps 15% - 20% of earnings, and supplementing this dividend with an annual special dividend based on the board's evaluation of the year's performance, capital requirements, and outlook. Banks using such a policy have the luxury of foregoing special dividends when circumstances warrant, while preserving the regular dividend. If the bank uses a special dividend, it must clearly communicate the policy to shareholders. This can be an effective means of preserving capital; however shareholders often become accustomed to regular special dividends.

» **When should a bank consider cutting the dividend?** When a bank needs capital the most (when earnings are depressed or nonexistent), reducing the dividend, or eliminating it entirely, may be prudent. Unfortunately, lowering the dividend may not provide a sufficient level of capital, because earnings are impaired. Another reason the dividend might be lowered is that the bank's primary regulatory agency orders elimination of the dividend payment until the financial problems are corrected.

One problem with eliminating dividends is that the bank is effectively admitting that the outlook for earnings is bleak. Creating this perception among shareholders can only serve to reduce the shares' liquidity and value. If the bank is having severe problems, this may be happening anyway. However, eliminating the dividend in order to raise capital is probably not a prudent policy for a healthy bank with a normal or near normal return on equity.

CHAPTER 12

SUB-CHAPTER S CONVERSIONS

According to the FDIC, 2,505 banks had elected to be taxed as S corporations at September 30, 2008, representing approximately 30% of all banks.[20] This chapter discusses what an S election is, why S elections have become popular, and the advantages and disadvantages of the election.

OVERVIEW

An S election represents a change in a bank's tax status. When a bank elects S corporation status, it opts to become taxed under Subchapter S of the U.S. Tax Code, instead of Subchapter C of the Code. When taxed as a C corporation, the bank pays federal income taxes on its taxable income. By making the S election, the bank no longer pays federal income tax itself. The tax liability does not disappear altogether, though. Instead, the tax liability passes through to the shareholders. This means that the bank's tax liability becomes the obligation of the bank's shareholders. The bank ordinarily intends to distribute enough cash to the shareholders to enable them to satisfy the tax liability, but there are no guarantees this will happen.

The following tables show what happens when a bank makes an S election (assuming that the federal and personal tax rates are identical at 35%). As shown, the bank no longer incurs any federal tax liability following the S election. Instead, the $350 tax obligation simply passes through to the shareholders.

Bank Perspective		**C Corp.**	**S Corp.**
Pre-Tax income		$1,000	$1,000
Federal Income Tax	35%	(350)	0
After-Tax Income		**$650**	**$1,000**
Shareholder Perspective		**C Corp.**	**S Corp.**
Taxable Income		0	$1,000
Pass-Through Tax Liability	35%	0	$350

In the preceding table, the bank's pre-tax income generated a $350 tax obligation, regardless of whether the bank was taxed as a C or S corporation. In the C corporation scenario, the bank directly paid the tax obligation to the government. In the S corporation alternative, the shareholders paid the taxes due on the bank's earnings. Since the taxes due remain constant at $350 regardless of whether the bank elects S corporation status or not, what incentive exists for banks to elect S corporation status?

Advantages

The S election creates two primary tax advantages relative to C corporations.

1. **Dividends paid by a C Corporation are taxable to the shareholders.** However, shareholders in an S corporation incur no tax liability beyond the taxes on their pro rata share of the S corporation's taxable income.

2. **In a C Corporation, a shareholder's tax basis generally remains constant during the period the shareholder holds the investment.** However, S corporation shareholders benefit because their tax basis increases to the extent that the bank retains earnings. This may reduce the capital gains taxes payable when a shareholder sells shares of the bank's stock.

The best way to illustrate the first tax advantage is with an example.

Bank Perspective		**C Corp.**	**S Corp.**
Pre-Tax income		$1,000	$1,000
Federal Income Tax	35%	(350)	0
After-Tax Income		**$650**	**$1,000**
Shareholder Dividends/Distributions		**$200**	**$550**
Amount Retained by Bank		**$450**	**$450**
Pass-Through Tax Liability		**C Corp.**	**S Corp.**
Taxable Income		$1,000	$1,000
Pass-Through Tax Liability	**35%**	**0**	**$350**
Shareholder Perspective		**C Corp.**	**S Corp.**
Shareholder Dividends/Distributions		$200	$550
Taxes on Dividends	15%	(30)	0
Pass-Through Tax Liability		0	(350)
After-Tax Cash Flow to Shareholders		**$170**	**$200**

In the C corporation scenario, the bank pays $200 of dividends to shareholders. After the shareholders pay taxes on these dividends (at a 15% tax rate on dividends), the shareholders will have after-tax cash flow of $170 from their investment. Assume, instead, that the bank elects S corporation status. In this case, the shareholders owe taxes of $350 (35% of the bank's $1,000 pre-tax income), but the bank makes distributions of $550.[21] This leaves the shareholders with $200 of after-tax cash flow. No further taxes are owed on the $200. In fact, for any amount of distributions between zero and $1,000 (the bank's pre-tax earnings), the shareholders generally face a tax liability of $350. By electing S corporation status, shareholders increase their after-tax cash flow from $170 to $200, an 18% increase.

Disadvantages

Given the aforementioned tax benefits, why wouldn't every bank elect S corporation status? Several potential disadvantages of the election exist.

» **Limitations exist on the type and number of shareholders that may hold stock in an S corporation.** If the bank currently has too many shareholders, a transaction that "squeezes out" certain shareholders may be necessary in order to make the election. This gives rise to the risk that shareholders might sue, demanding a greater amount for their shares than offered by the bank.

» **S elections can increase the risk associated with an investment in the bank.** For instance, assume that the bank reports a pre-tax loss of $1,000. If the bank is taxed as a C corporation, it generally records a tax benefit related to the loss, and, the bank's retained earnings fall by only $650 (the $1,000 pre-tax loss minus a $350 tax benefit, assuming a 35% tax rate). However, if the bank is taxed as an S corporation, it records no tax benefit in its books, and the entire $1,000 pre-tax loss flows through retained earnings. Thus, in the event that a loss occurs, the S corporation's capital account will be $350 less than the capital account of a similarly situated C corporation (which is equal to the amount of the tax benefit recorded by the C corporation). In the event that the losses are significant to the bank, the adverse capital treatment of an S corporation can prove material.

» **In addition to the preceding effect on capital, the S corporation bank may have taxable income (thereby creating a tax obligation on the part of the bank's shareholders) but a net loss for book purposes.** For instance, this could occur because loan loss provisions in excess of actual loan losses may not be tax deductible. This situation could create a highly negative outcome for the bank's shareholders. The shareholders may face a personal tax liability but the bank's capital position may limit its ability to make distributions to the shareholders.

» **To minimize risks associated with an S election, the board of directors and management may adopt a more conservative management style for the S corporation bank than the C corporation bank.** For instance, higher capital ratios may be desirable. In addition, the bank may adopt stricter underwriting requirements or maintain a lower loan/deposit ratio to reduce the risk of losses.

» **Regulators can order the bank to suspend dividend payments, irrespective of the shareholder tax liability.** Regulators have significant legal authority to do this. You should remember their objective is to protect the safety and soundness of the institution, and they have no obligation to the shareholders.

» **The advantages of S elections depend to some degree on the relationship between corporate, personal, and dividend tax rates.** In the future, changes in the relationship between these tax rates could make S elections less desirable. For instance, a reduction in the C corporation tax rate, coupled with personal tax rate increases, could reduce or eliminate the benefits associated with an S election.

» **Certain one-time costs associated with an S election exist.** For example, a bank generally must write off its deferred tax asset (if it has one) upon the S election. This write-off reduces earnings and capital in the year it occurs.

» **The bank may still face federal income taxes on certain assets sold within ten years of the S election.** This is referred to as the built-in gains tax.

» **The S election may limit access to growth capital.** This growth capital is needed to resolve financial problems.

Summary

S corporation elections may be an attractive alternative for banks, but a careful examination of the advantages and disadvantages is necessary. Banks with relatively low balance sheet growth and high profitability often make the best candidates for S elections, because these banks have the capacity to distribute a large portion of their earnings. On the other hand, an S election would be less beneficial for other types of banks. For instance, banks that intend to pursue acquisitions or that have potentially volatile earnings may be served better by remaining C corporations.

If your bank decides to make an S election, the process typically is more complicated than simply checking a box on a tax filing. Instead, a number of professionals may need to be involved to ensure the bank's goals are achieved.

» **The bank's corporate attorney will likely be involved throughout the process.** The attorney will assist with any issues related to shareholders that do not qualify as S corporation shareholders (for instance, by negotiating a voluntary repurchase or structuring an involuntary transaction), drafting any necessary proxy statements distributed to the shareholders, and creating the shareholder agreement that restricts the sale of the bank's shares to preserve the S election.

» **The bank's tax accountant or tax attorney will also have an important role.** This includes analyzing the shareholder base to determine which shareholders may not qualify as S corporation shareholders and considering any specific tax issues relevant to the bank.

» **A business appraiser can have several roles in a Subchapter S election.** First, the bank may require an appraisal of its stock prior to the S election for purposes of the built-in gains tax that may arise if the bank is eventually sold. Second, appraisals often are necessary when repurchasing stock from non-qualifying shareholders, whether the transaction is voluntary or involuntary. Third, a fairness opinion may be needed to determine the fairness of the squeeze out transaction to the bank's shareholders or one specific group of shareholders, such as the ESOP.

FINANCIAL ISSUES

In a preceding table, we created an example whereby a C corporation earned $650 after-tax, while a similarly situated S corporation reported $1,000 of net income. Assuming that the bank is worth 12x earnings, this would mean that the C corporation is worth $7,800 ($650 x 12), while the S corporation is worth $12,000 ($1,000 x 12), if both are valued at the same multiple. Thus, by making the S election, the bank seems to have increased its value by 54%, simply by changing its tax status. Can this be right? The answer is a resounding "no."

Keep in mind that the tax liability did not disappear upon the S election; instead, the party directly responsible for writing a check to the federal government shifted from the bank itself to its shareholders. To avoid making its shareholders unhappy, the bank ordinarily distributes enough cash to allow the shareholders to satisfy the pass-through tax obligation. As a result, the bank ends up in virtually the same capital and cash flow position, whether it makes the S election or not. To understand this, consider the following.

» In the C corporation example, the bank wrote the federal government a check for $350 to cover the tax obligation. It also sent checks to the shareholders for $200 as dividends.

» In the S corporation scenario, the bank sent checks to the shareholders to cover the $350 tax obligation. The bank also sent the shareholders additional checks for $200 to provide a supplementary "economic" dividend, similar to the C corporation scenario.

» At the end of the day, after paying taxes and shareholder dividends, the bank retains $450 regardless of whether it makes the S election or not. The following table shows this computation.

Bank Perspective			
Pre-Tax income		$1,000	$1,000
- Federal Income Tax	35%	(350)	0
- Shareholder Dividends/Distributions		(200)	(550)
= **Increase in Retained Earnings**		**$450**	**$450**

Since the bank's retained earnings increase by about the same amount regardless of whether it makes an S election or not, directors should not expect the S election itself to enhance the value of the bank as a whole. However, the elimination of the double taxation of dividends (meaning that C corporation shareholders also pay taxes on dividends after the bank has paid taxes on its earnings) can affect the value of a shareholders' investment favorably to some degree. Yet, any analysis of the benefits of the S election must also consider the disadvantages, such as potentially higher risk and the more limited market within which to sell the investment in an S corporation as compared to a C corporation. The impact of an S election on value depends on the facts and circumstances of each bank, but the value enhancement, if any, will be much lower than the 54% calculated previously in our example, which simplistically applied a 12x price/earnings multiple to both the S corporation's and C corporation's reported net income.

SECTION FIVE

FINANCIAL REPORTING

> I have no use for bodyguards, but I have a very specific use for two highly trained accountants.
>
> Elvis Presley
> *Musician*

This section provides an overview of how valuation analyses have penetrated accounting principles, and details a number of accounting issues for which external valuation assistance is frequently required. We hope that this section provides sufficient information to foresee potential accounting issues that might arise at your bank. Additionally, a general understanding of this topic provides a reasonable basis to determine whether any valuation services provided to your bank reflect a comprehensive understanding of your bank, accounting rules, and their application to the financial services industry.

Chapter 13 defines fair value from an accounting perspective and relates its application to investments such as loans and securities. Chapter 14 focuses more specifically on fair value issues that arise in an acquisition, in particular the determination of the fair value of depository customer relationships and goodwill impairment testing. Chapter 15 provides an overview of the accounting rules related to share-based compensation and identifies the critical inputs for directors to focus on when assessing management or their appraiser's fair value measurements. The appropriateness of fair value measurements is important for both accounting purposes (to determine compensation expense) and compensation purposes.

CHAPTER 13

FAIR VALUE ACCOUNTING

For years, accountants have weighed the advantages and disadvantages of the two primary accounting models – historical cost and fair value. These debates are couched in terms of the relevance and reliability of the two models. Relevance means that the accounting information provides meaningful information to investors for use in analyzing the bank. Reliability relates to the extent to which the accounting information is verifiable and faithfully represents what it purports to represent.

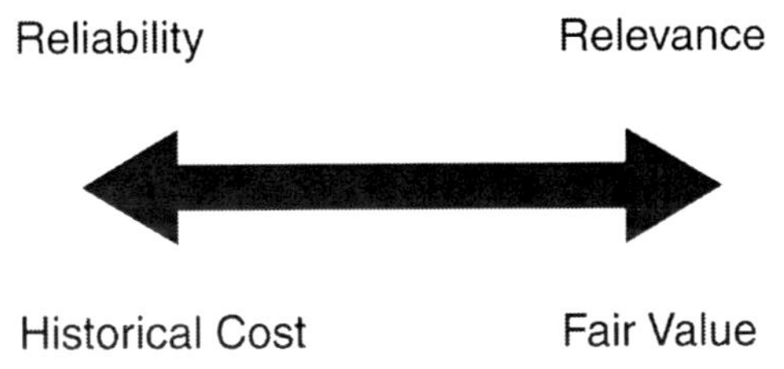

OVERVIEW

Historical cost means that an asset is recorded on the balance sheet at its original cost. As an example, consider the purchase of land. This method scores highly on reliability, because the bank can easily identify the cost of the land from its purchasing records. However, this method suffers in terms of relevance, because in future years the value of the land may diverge from its cost. Despite the appreciation, the bank would continue to carry the land on its balance sheet at cost until it elects to sell the land. Investors are more likely concerned with the current value of the land than its historical cost.

For the fair value model, the opposite holds true. That is, fair value information often is more relevant to investors but may be less reliable. The diminished reliability often results from difficulties in verifying such information, meaning that determinations of fair value are predicated on assumptions and may not really reflect the value that the bank actually may receive from selling the asset.

This tug-of-war between historical cost and fair value has persisted for years, but newer accounting pronouncements generally have expressed a desire for fair value information. While the accounting for some assets has shifted to the fair value model, accounting for other assets remains rooted in the historical cost model. The result is a potentially confusing hodgepodge of accounting guidance.

As indicated in the following table, some assets are carried at historical cost, others at fair value, and yet more under something of a hybrid approach.

	Historical Cost	Fair Value	Hybrid
Loans Held-for-Investment	X		
Loans Held-for-Sale		X	
Securities with Determinable Market Values		X	
Securities without Determinable Market Values	X		
Premises & Equipment	X		
Assets Acquired in Business Combinations			X

DEFINITION OF FAIR VALUE

Paragraph 5 of Financial Accounting Standard 157 defines fair value as:

> "Fair value is the price that would be received to sell an asset or paid to transfer a liability in an orderly transaction between market participants at the measurement date."[22]

In Chapter 2, we discussed a concept of fair value that applies in certain corporate transactions affecting the rights of minority shareholders. We termed this statutory fair value because it arises from the corporate law statutes applicable to the bank. However, fair value as discussed in this section is a very different concept that derives from the accounting literature. Throughout

Chapters 13 through 15, when we refer to fair value, we refer to fair value as defined by certain accounting standards, not statutory fair value.

To create a more uniform understanding of the definition, the accounting standards further define each of the constituent elements of fair value.

» The "**price**" represents an amount that would be received upon selling the asset. This means that fair value represents an exit price. Thus, the entry price, such as the amount the bank paid to acquire the asset, is not necessarily germane to determining fair value, nor is the price at which the bank is willing to sell.

» An "**orderly transaction**" means that the transaction is not a forced transaction (such as a liquidation or distress sale) and further assumes that a typical and customary marketing process for the asset occurs. The meaning of the term "orderly transaction" has become quite controversial for some assets, such as subprime mortgage-backed securities. Additional accounting guidance clarifies that one's belief that a market price is irrational is insufficient reason to discard such market pricing as indicative of a forced transaction.[23] Thus, even an "irrational" market price nevertheless would represent the fair value of such asset.

» A "**market participant**" is a party that is knowledgeable about the asset, able to acquire the asset, and willing to transact for the asset, but not compelled to do so. A certain asset may have value to a particular bank that exceeds its value to other banks that would be potential buyers of that asset. In that case, the fair value of the asset is its value in the broader market and not its value to one particular buyer.

FINANCIAL ISSUES

Securities

For bond investments, banks generally receive pricing information from correspondent banks or broker/dealers. But, for certain investments or in volatile market environments, pricing information from traditional sources may not be available. In this case, a bank may need to look to a valuation specialist for assistance.

If no market quotation exists for a certain bond, how should the bank proceed in determining its value? The first option may be to determine whether any market information exists for bonds with similar characteristics. If not, the only option in many cases is a pricing model. This pricing model would use, for instance, information on defaults, prepayments, and discount rates to determine the value. Importantly, these assumptions should be consistent with those used by marketplace participants, not necessarily the bank's own estimates.

For bonds with an impaired market, a final caveat is in order. For the securities that comprise most of a bank's bond portfolio, declines in value ordinarily are deemed to be temporary. This means that ultimately the bank collects the interest and principal payments if it holds the bonds to maturity, implying that the decline in value is due to changes in interest rates rather than the credit quality of the bond. Alternatively, one reason that an impaired market may exist is that investor demand for the bond has disappeared due to the bond's perceived risk. In this case, the bank would need to reevaluate its assumptions as to whether the principal and interest payments will be collected in a timely manner. Depending on the outcome of this review, the bond may be deemed "other than temporarily" impaired, which results in a write-down of the bond through the bank's income statement.

If a bank holds securities for which a market price is not readily available, it should consult with its auditors and potentially its regulators to determine other forms of acceptable valuation evidence and to ascertain whether "other than temporary" impairment may exist. The auditors and/or regulators may require a valuation specialist to render an independent opinion as to the fair value of the security.

Loans

There are three situations in which a bank may need to determine the fair value of its loans.

» **Loans Held-for-Sale.** If a bank holds loans with the intent to sell them, these loans are accounted for at the lower of cost or market, where "market" is defined as the loans' fair value. The most common example of loans held-for-sale is mortgage loans awaiting sale into the secondary market. Such loans often have a committed take-out price from an investor and therefore ordinarily do not present any significant valuation issues. If the investor fails to honor its take-out commitment, however, then the bank may have to determine the fair value independently.

» **Loans Held-for-Investment.** The loans that a bank holds in its loan portfolio are stated at the principal amount outstanding, less the allowance for loan losses. Accounting standards require banks to provide the fair value of loans in the footnotes to the financial statements.

» **Loans Acquired in Business Combinations.** When a bank acquires another bank, the acquiring bank records the purchased loans at their fair value, not the amount reported on the acquired bank's books. Thus, the acquiring bank ends up with an amalgamation of loans recorded at fair value (the loans purchased in the acquisition) and at the principal amount outstanding (the existing loan portfolio of the acquiring bank).

In determining the fair value of loans, accounting standards suggest that banks should look first to the prices for similar loans that are observable in the marketplace. For most of the loans held by community banks, such market information is not readily available. Absent any market data, the bank's only recourse is to use a valuation model.

The most significant factors bearing on the valuation of a loan portfolio include:

» **Fixed or Floating Interest Rates.** For floating rate loans, the fair value of the loans generally equals the principal amount outstanding, according to SFAS 107.[24] Therefore, fair value determination generally focuses on fixed rate loans.

» **Prepayments.** While fixed rate loans have stated maturities, the borrower usually has the right to prepay the loan, sometimes for a fee. In this case, the valuation process requires estimating the loan's prepayment rates to better forecast the time period over which the loan will remain outstanding. Loan prepayments can be good or bad. In periods of rising rates, prepayments often are desirable, because the bank can use the funds to invest in loans bearing interest at the higher market rates. More often, however, loan prepayments are a negative factor, because borrowers only have an incentive to prepay when interest rates are falling – which is exactly when banks would prefer for the loan to remain outstanding.

» **Credit Risk.** Credit risk is a complicated factor because it lies at the intersection of several accounting issues. Loan portfolio valuations often are prepared on a "credit neutral" basis, meaning that any deterioration in the quality of the loan between its origination date and the valuation date is captured in the loan loss reserve associated with that loan rather than the fair value of the loan.

» **Discount Rate.** The discount rate for the loans should be based on returns currently required by market participants. In practice, this is difficult to ascertain for many loan types. One alternative is to look to the rates at which the bank presently issues similar loans and assume that other banks competing in the marketplace would be willing to enter into loans on similar terms.

Determining the fair value of a loan portfolio requires significant detail regarding each loan in the portfolio. Individual loans are typically grouped into pools based on similar type, maturity, and rate (such as consumer loans with 12-to-24 months to maturity and interest rates of 6% to 7%, commercial loans with 36-to-48 months to maturity and interest rates of 7% to 8%, etc.).

The valuation model then projects the cash flows associated with each pool of loans, which are then discounted to the present value at the current rate required by market participants. By adding the values indicated for each pool, the bank can determine the fair value of the entire portfolio.

Valuations of loans may be needed periodically (for the footnote disclosures required in a bank's annual audited financial statements) or in specific circumstances (such as the acquisition of another bank). Auditors may require independent valuations for loans acquired in business combinations but not for the periodic disclosures in financial statements. You should understand, therefore, the requirements of the bank's auditing firm. Regardless of whether an independent valuation is required or not, board members should understand the key assumptions influencing the value of the loan portfolio – the types of loans (fixed vs. floating), the prepayment rates, the treatment of credit risk, and the discount rates.

CHAPTER 14

FAIR VALUE ACCOUNTING IN BUSINESS COMBINATIONS

When a bank makes an acquisition of another entity, accounting issues are not the foremost consideration in the minds of directors who are often focused on achieving a successful deal for the bank's shareholders. Nevertheless, the accounting for the transaction may have an impact on the bank's balance sheet and income statement for years to come.

When a bank acquires another entity (either a bank or a non-banking company), the buyer is required to determine the fair value of all the assets acquired and liabilities assumed. This allocation process includes all assets acquired, whether or not these assets are recognized on the seller's balance sheet.

What is an example of an asset that lies unrecognized on the seller's balance sheet but that a buyer would recognize? Consider the trademark for Coca-Cola. Based on historical cost accounting, Coca-Cola's balance sheet does not incorporate the fair value of the Coca-Cola trademark. If, however, Pepsi were to acquire Coca-Cola, then Pepsi would need to determine the fair value of the Coca-Cola trademark and record such value on its balance sheet. Generally, the Coca-Cola trademark and other previously unrecognized assets acquired in business combinations fall into the category of "intangible" assets.

In banking acquisitions, the most significant intangible assets fall into the category of so-called "customer relationship" intangible assets. These intangible assets represent the benefits accruing to the bank from the customers' repeat patronage. For instance, if a bank acquires an insurance agency, then the stream of future income generated from policy renewals is an example of a customer relationship intangible asset.

The following table gives examples of assets and liabilities often recorded by banks at fair value upon an acquisition.

Assets Recorded at Fair Value	Liabilities Recorded at Fair Value
Securities	Certificates of Deposits
Loans	Federal Home Loan Bank Advances
Premises & Equipment	Trust Preferred Securities
Indentifiable Intangible Assets	
Depositor Customer Relationships (Core Deposits)	
Borrower Relationships	
Insurance Customer Relationships (Expirations)	
Trust/Asset Management Customer Relationships	
Merchant Processing Customer Relationships	
Employment Agreements	

The determination of the fair value of securities and loans was discussed in the previous chapter, and that discussion holds true in the context of both business combinations and periodic financial reporting. The preceding table lists several types of intangible assets that must be recognized. Similarities exist between the valuation of depositor customer relationships and other types of customer relationships, although the scope of this chapter is limited to depositor customer relationships.

DEPOSITOR CUSTOMER RELATIONSHIPS

Overview

A depositor customer relationship intangible asset was formerly known as a "core deposit intangible asset," but the current accounting standards use the term "depositor relationship." Core deposit valuation first arose as a significant issue in the 1980s when, for tax reasons, banks argued that core deposits constituted a significant part of the value of an acquired bank. The core deposit amount could be deducted for income tax purposes, resulting in numerous Internal Revenue Service challenges to banks' core deposit intangible asset valuations. Changes in the tax rules eventually laid to rest the tax issues related to core deposit valuation and the amortization of the core deposit intangible asset, but changes to the accounting rules in 2001 resuscitated core deposit (or depositor relationship) intangible assets as a significant issue for banks.

Financial Issues

Deposits provide a relatively stable source of funding that a bank can invest in interest earning assets, like loans, or use to replace more expensive borrowings, such as Federal Home Loan Bank advances. Deposits also may provide income in the form of fees, such as insufficient funds charges. So the value of a depositor customer relationship derives from these characteristics of deposits.

Valuing a depositor relationship requires specifying:

» **The Interest Spread.** The interest spread is the difference between the cost of the deposits and either the yield on a portfolio of assets that could be funded by the deposits, or the cost of wholesale borrowings that could be replaced by the deposits.

» **Fees.** The deposit fees are those typically generated by banks, such as account charges and insufficient funds fees.

» **Operating Expenses.** Maintaining the deposits requires expenditures on everything from people to premises to postage.

» **Attrition Rate.** Depositor relationships have finite lives. An important component of the valuation analysis is to estimate just how finite the life may be – will it be two years, or five years, or ten years? This life, in turn, determines how long the accounts will produce economic benefits to the acquirer. To estimate the life of the depositor relationships, appraisers use an attrition rate, which measures the number of accounts or the dollar value of accounts projected to close in each year.

» **Discount Rate.** Using the estimates as to the interest spread, fees, operating expenses, and attrition, the valuation analysis projects the future cash flows generated by the depositor relationships. These cash flows are then discounted to the present to determine the fair value of the depositor customer relationships. The discount rate used is usually based on the discount rate for equity, rather than debt.

Once the bank determines the fair value of the acquired bank's depositor relationships, this value is recorded on the acquirer's balance sheet. Then, the value is written off over the life of the depositor relationships through the income statement. Thus, the amount assigned to the depositor relationship intangible asset, like all intangible assets with a definite life, ultimately affects the bank's reported net income in subsequent years.

Auditors typically expect independent valuations of intangible assets because of the materiality of acquisitions. If a bank undertakes an acquisition, coordination is needed among the acquiring bank's management, the target bank's management, auditors, and valuation specialists to develop the required information and complete the valuations. Accounting and valuation issues related to business combinations continue to evolve; thus, directors should be prepared for a potentially complicated process.

GOODWILL

Overview

Even after the bank identifies and determines the fair value of all the assets and liabilities acquired in the business combination, the price paid to acquire the target company is unlikely to equal the fair value of the assets, net of the fair value of liabilities. Comparing the purchase price with the fair value of the assets (both tangible and intangible), net of liabilities, gives rise to another intangible asset, goodwill. Goodwill is a residual asset, meaning that it cannot be calculated directly. Instead, it "falls out" based on the relationship between the purchase price and the fair value of the assets and liabilities acquired.

The following table indicates the derivation of goodwill.

	Book Value	Fair Value
Securities	$20	$20
Loans	75	78
Other Assets	5	5
Depositor Customer Relationships	0	3
Goodwill	0	6
Total Assets	**$100**	**$112**
Demand Deposits	$60	$60
Time Deposits	25	26
Federal Home Loan Bank Advances	5	6
Total Liabilities	$90	$92
Total Equity	$10	$20
Total Liabilities & Equity	**$100**	**$112**

The table assumes that a bank acquires another bank with $10 of book equity for a purchase price of $20. Initially, the acquiring bank determines the fair value of the loans, time deposits, and Federal Home Loan Bank advances. Next, the bank calculates the value of the identifiable intangible assets, such as the depositor relationships. Goodwill ($6 in the preceding table) is the amount necessary to "plug" the balance sheet, such that the fair value of the assets acquired equals the fair value of the liabilities assumed plus the purchase price.

Unlike the depositor relationship intangible asset, goodwill is not written off over time through the income statement. Instead, it remains at a constant amount on the balance sheet, unless it is deemed to be impaired. This different treatment of goodwill versus intangible assets, such as depositor relationships, arises from the fact that goodwill has no determinable life.

Goodwill Impairment Testing

The potential for goodwill impairment following an acquisition is a risk of which directors should be aware. Goodwill must be tested for impairment at least annually. The goodwill impairment testing process involves the following key steps.

» **First, the bank must determine what to test for impairment.** The accounting standards specify that the bank must group its operations into "reporting units" and test goodwill at the reporting unit level. A reporting unit can be either the entire bank or a division of the bank. A bank may merge an acquisition into one of its existing reporting units, rather than treat the acquisition as a separate reporting unit. To some extent, the risk of impairment depends on how the bank defines its reporting units. For instance, if the acquired company resides within its own separate reporting unit, then the risk of impairment is likely greater than if the acquired company is subsumed into one of the bank's other reporting units that have little goodwill.

» **Second, the bank must determine the fair value of each reporting unit.** The accounting guidance specifies that the basis for the fair value determination is the reporting unit as a whole. Thus, the accounting literature appears to equate the fair value of the reporting unit to a controlling interest value, not the value of a minority interest in the reporting unit. With this theoretical basis, fair value can be determined using some variation of the cost (asset-based), market, and income approaches (see Chapter 2 for discussion of the three general approaches to valuation). Ordinarily, the market and income approaches predominate in determining fair value. For publicly traded companies, one test of reasonableness of the fair value estimates is to compare the fair value of all of the bank's reporting units to the bank's market capitalization.

» **Third, the bank compares the fair value of the reporting unit to its carrying value, which is usually the reporting unit's total equity.** If the fair value of the reporting unit exceeds its carrying value, then no impairment is deemed to exist. Continuing the previous example, assume that the acquired entity constitutes a separate reporting unit. Thus, the reporting unit has equity (and a carrying value) of $20. If the fair value of the reporting unit is $25, then no impairment would exist.

However, if the fair value of the reporting unit is less than its carrying value, then impairment likely exists. Calculating the amount of the impairment involves a complicated process of determining the fair value of all of the assets and liabilities of the reporting unit. The amount of the goodwill impairment loss, if any, depends on these calculations. The impairment loss is recorded as an operating expense on the bank's income statement. While the impairment affects the bank's net income, it has no impact on the bank's regulatory capital, because goodwill is already excluded in calculating capital.

Financial Issues

Issues related to goodwill require significant assumptions, and the accounting for goodwill is often listed as a critical accounting policy in publicly traded companies' SEC filings. Directors should be aware of the areas that require the most significant judgments, which are:

» The determination of the reporting units.

» The determination of the fair value of the reporting unit(s). In addition to market data, such as valuation multiples, this requires data provided by management, such as financial forecasts and projections.

Given the materiality of goodwill to many banks and the knowledge required regarding valuation techniques in the context of fair value, auditors often prefer an independent impairment test to one prepared internally. Whether it is prepared internally or externally, directors should become comfortable that the goodwill impairment test is prepared using reasonable estimates as to the future performance of the reporting unit and how the market values similar entities.

CHAPTER 15

SHARE-BASED COMPENSATION

Another area where valuation analyses have penetrated accounting is the accounting for share-based compensation, such as stock options. Formerly, accounting rules permitted companies to record no compensation expense for stock options meeting certain criteria. This favorable accounting treatment of stock options was believed by some to have led to excessive stock option grants by companies and/or an excessive emphasis on stock options over other forms of compensation. In 2005, new accounting rules were introduced that mandated that companies expense the cost of stock option grants as well as other forms of share-based compensation.

Under current accounting rules, a bank would determine, as of the grant date, the fair value of the stock options or other share-based compensation. The fair value of such compensation then would be expensed over the estimated life of the options or other compensation.

OVERVIEW

Previously, we cited an accounting standard that defined fair value as, "the price that would be received to sell an asset or paid to transfer a liability in an orderly transaction between market participants at the measurement date." Interestingly, the accounting standard for share-based compensation adopts the term "fair value," but share-based compensation specifically is excluded from the accounting standard that sets forth and defines the term "fair value." Thus, the determination of fair value for stock options exists almost in a separate universe, not governed by the laws of fair value affecting the valuations of other assets and liabilities.

The universe in which banks derive the fair value of stock options has many complicated rules. The accounting standards recognize that two general models exist to value stock options – the Black/Scholes model and the binomial lattice model. Without delving into the specifics, trust us that these two models derive almost identical values for non-dividend paying stocks and very similar values for dividend-paying stocks.

FINANCIAL ISSUES

In practice, the Black/Scholes pricing model appears to be used most often, so this discussion focuses on this model over the binomial lattice model. The Black/Scholes model compresses a complex pricing formula into an equation with six variables.

1. **Risk-Free Interest Rate.** As the risk-free interest rate (such as the Treasury rate) increases, the value of the option increases. With a higher interest rate, the option-holder would rather hold the option and avoid paying the exercise price than forfeit the ability to earn the risk-free rate by exercising the option (and paying the exercise price).

2. **Time to Maturity.** As the time to maturity increases, the value of the option increases. With a longer life, there is a greater probability that the option will be valuable to a holder.

3. **Volatility.** Volatility relates to the movement in the bank's stock price. As volatility increases, the value of the option increases. This may be a somewhat surprising result, but greater volatility implies a higher probability that the stock price ultimately will exceed the option's exercise price. This makes the option more valuable.

4. **Exercise Price.** As the exercise price increases, the value of the stock option decreases. This occurs because the option is more likely to expire worthless (at a higher exercise price).

5. **Dividend Yield.** As the dividend on the underlying common stock increases, the value of the stock option decreases. If a stock pays a dividend, an investor may prefer to hold the stock and receive the dividend versus holding the option and forgoing the dividend. Thus, the dividend yield and option value are inversely correlated.

6. **Market Value of the Stock.** Holding all the preceding factors constant, an option on a more valuable stock is worth more than an option on a less valuable stock, because the potential payoff is higher (in dollar terms). Thus, as the market value of the stock increases, the value of the option increases.

Of these six inputs into the Black/Scholes model, four are susceptible to relatively precise estimates (the market value of the stock for publicly traded companies, the risk-free interest rate, the exercise price, and the dividend yield). That leaves two inputs where a range of estimates conceivably could exist – volatility and the time to maturity.

To estimate volatility, companies often calculate the volatility of their own stock market prices. While this method is used frequently in practice, it has one important shortcoming. Namely, volatility should be forward-looking, and historical estimates of volatility may not be representative of future volatility. The accounting rules allow privately held banks to assume 0% volatility, rather than create some sort of market proxy to estimate their volatility.

The accounting standard related to share-based compensation provides significant guidance on estimating the time to maturity of the option. Unlike options that trade in the marketplace, many options issued by banks have vesting requirements that mean some of the options will never be exercised. For instance, if a QFDR event occurs (that is, the employee quits, is fired, dies, or retires), the employee may forfeit his or her options. To recognize this behavior, the accounting rules allow banks to shorten the expected life of the options based on estimates of expected forfeitures.

Valuations related to the fair value of stock options or any other share-based compensation arrangements are inherently complex, as is the entirety of the accounting related to stock-based compensation. By focusing on a few key inputs (such as the volatility and expected life estimates), directors can assess the fair value measurements made by management more competently. The appropriateness of the fair value measurements is important for both accounting purposes (through the determination of compensation expense) and compensation purposes (by ensuring that the value of the options granted will encourage the grantees to accomplish the board's objectives but not cause excessive dilution to existing shareholders).

SECTION SIX

STATUTORY & LEGAL CONCEPTS

Anybody who thinks talk is cheap should get some legal advice.

Franklin P. Jones
Businessman

This section provides an overview of a number of valuation services that might be helpful should a litigated situation involving your bank arise, focusing specifically on two litigated situations that we frequently encounter in our practice. Chapter 16 provides an overview of the valuation services that might be helpful should litigation arise. Chapter 17 focuses on transactions that might trigger dissenters' rights litigation. Chapter 18 provides a few useful items to consider should a personal divorce of a shareholder occur. This topic is included because we have witnessed situations where a bank has been adversely affected, particularly if no public market for the bank's stock exists.

CHAPTER 16

A PRIMER ON LITIGATION

Valuation advisory services can provide the thoughtful documentation required to conduct those transactions that may be scrutinized by regulators, courts, tax collectors, and a myriad of other lurking adversaries. Moving beyond the typical compliance issues, valuation services can be useful in the litigation arena, since value is the centerpiece of much business and personal litigation. The high-stakes, hard-to-quantify issues of litigation always are challenged aggressively. In essence, an expert analyst should do three essential things to address any question of value, whether in litigation or a compliance environment.

» Focus on relevant information.

» Draw conclusions that have economic substance.

» Articulate the reasonableness of conclusions in a manner that appeals to common sense.

A qualified expert has practical experience dealing with real problems of companies and individuals. A business appraiser should be able to define the valuation issues, assemble the relevant information, and quantify the financial aspects of a case. Moreover, an expert should be able to communicate the soundness of conclusions convincingly.

The following list provides an overview of areas of litigation that are most likely to require the type of support that a business valuation professional can provide.

- » Trial support
- » Business damages
- » Buy-sell agreements
- » Securities fraud analyses
- » Goodwill analyses
- » Family law and marital dissolution
- » Blockage analyses
- » Fair value controversies
- » Tax-related controversies
- » ESOPs and other ERISA-related disputes
- » Bankruptcy and corporate reorganization
- » Mediation or arbitration
- » M&A advisory engagements

CHAPTER 17

STATUTORY FAIR VALUE

Let us begin with the following statement: Mercer Capital does not practice law and nothing in this chapter should be interpreted as providing legal advice. Our objective is to give the reader information from a business appraisal perspective, gleaned from involvement in numerous litigated cases and provided valuations in scores more cases over the past 25 years. Our hope is that you use this chapter as a guide to developing your own questions as you meet with legal counsel, valuation consultants, and other financial advisors. This is a complex topic, hence this chapter can provide only a brief overview. Each state law may have slightly different terms; however, we have chosen to use the most common ones for this book. Seek the best possible legal advice when you entertain a transaction which can trigger dissenters' rights.

OVERVIEW

From a statutory perspective, fair value is a legal term which arises when a business is engaging in some type of corporate reorganization. The reorganization plan may trigger dissenters' rights, which means a shareholder can vote against the plan and demand fair value (or some equivalent term) to be paid in cash.

Both the bank and the shareholder develop their own ideas of the appropriate fair value. Each point of view requires a decision as to the proper level of value and the appropriate application of valuation methods to determine value at that level. At this point, referencing Chapter 2, which discusses the levels of value, may be helpful. The basis of disputes often is rooted as much in which level of value should be used as in the application of the valuation methods themselves.

Before we delve into the financial issues, we give consideration to two other perspectives: legal and emotional.

Legal Perspective

Corporate law affords companies the opportunity for various types of reorganizations. Shareholders do not have to be unanimous in their approval of the proposed action; however, those who dissent and perfect their rights under the law typically must be paid for their shares. The standard of value for valuation in this circumstance is most commonly fair value, with a few states opting for fair market value or fair cash value. A federal statute provides for market value in situations involving national banks. In every situation, the standard of value is stated in the statute or defined in varying degrees by court cases. When relying on court cases, these definitions may be somewhat opaque.

State law generally governs state chartered banks and bank holding companies, while Section 214a of the National Bank Act governs national banks. State and federal court decisions typically interpret and apply the laws, although in a few cases this may be the province of state banking regulators.

The statutes and interpretation of fair value have been fluid for the past 15 years. Laws have changed, court decisions have changed the interpretation of existing laws, and many states have court cases which better define their laws. Because the topic has been so fluid over time, geography, and jurisdiction, you must have a precise understanding of the transaction you are contemplating and an understanding of fair value as it exists in your jurisdiction at the time of the transaction. What some other bank or holding company did at some other time and place may be irrelevant to you.

From a lay person's perspective, definitions or interpretations of fair value can be found:

» In the statute (see the model code).

» In court decisions within your state.

» In court decisions from other states (Delaware is an example) which may influence the law within your state.

If the statute is not explicit, then your attorneys are going to rely on an interpretation of the court decisions. You should talk with them to understand how firm they are in their positions, since a different interpretation could lead to a significantly different conclusion of value.

Emotional Perspective

This may strike you as an unusual topic for a financial book; however, it is not. Dissenting shareholder activities are some of the most emotional and intensely litigated situations that we encounter. For a variety of reasons, transactions that elicit dissenting shareholder activities have many of the characteristics of a personal divorce.

The reasons for the intensity of emotion are as countless as the number of people who feel the emotions. We have heard bankers say:

» "These people never did anything to build the bank."

» "My family guaranteed loans to help the bank survive when they wouldn't."

» "I have worked countless hours to build this place; all they ever wanted was a dividend."

To the banker, we would say that all of these emotions are real, but irrelevant.

We have heard the dissenting shareholder say:

» "They never paid a dividend, even though they could."

» "Bankers always feel they have it made and never have to work as hard as we do."

» Or statements that begin, "when we were children...," or, "when my father ..."

To the shareholder, we would say that all of these emotions are real, but irrelevant.

Put simply, if litigation ensues, there will be some emotional fallout. None of this is said to discourage a legitimate transaction on the part of the bank or rightful dissent by a shareholder. It is written simply to inform you of the nature of these transactions.

FINANCIAL ISSUES

To repeat, fair value in a statutory matter has no meaning in valuation absent an understanding of the legal framework that provides guidance to the appraiser. Having said that, court decisions can be contradictory, dated in their use of valuation terminology, or unclear. Consulting with legal counsel is essential. In many cases opposing parties may argue simply that the law should be changed via a different court interpretation and may be successful. As noted previously, the situation is ever changing.

Fair value has been interpreted by courts at all three levels of value (control, marketable minority, and nonmarketable minority) and with some refinements within each of those categories. The appraiser's job is not to define fair value in your jurisdiction, but to apply valuation principles appropriately to the legal framework.

The board of directors often obtain an appraisal prior to initiating a transaction and rely upon it in making the decision to proceed. The corporate reorganization may take several more months to be completed. If there is dissent, most states place the valuation date at or near the day of the shareholder vote which affects the reorganization. Hence the "valuation date" (see Chapter 1) may have moved months away from the board meeting which originally approved the event. If litigation ensues between the company and the dissenting shareholders, it may not be resolved for several years.

The financial advisor may serve one or more functions. Primarily, the advisor provides appraisal services and/or a fairness opinion. The appraisal is an opinion of value of the stock and is used by the board of directors in setting a price to be offered to shareholders. A fairness opinion (discussed more fully in Chapter 10) addresses the fairness of the transaction from a financial point of view to a specific constituency that is affected by the transaction. Whether or not you need a fairness opinion is a decision that should be made after consultation with legal counsel.

Certain financial analyses are performed by bank personnel to answer the following questions.

» Will the bank have sufficient capital after the transaction for regulatory and business purposes?

» Will the bank holding company be able to service debt arising from the transaction?

» What is the pro forma effect on earnings and earnings per share for the remaining shareholders?

Banks are regulated companies. They must meet minimum standards of regulatory capital. They also must have adequate capital to sustain and grow the business. An analysis of capital adequacy is a critical piece of any study of financial feasibility. Bank directors must ask the following questions: What is the margin of error if the bank's valuation is not sustained in a court proceeding and a higher price must be paid for the shares? Do you have a backup plan such as additional debt or lower capital levels?

CHAPTER 18

DIVORCE OF A KEY SHAREHOLDER

A personal divorce is always a difficult situation. It can have an adverse impact on any small business, including a community bank. This is particularly true when there is no public market for the bank's stock. A full discussion of this topic is beyond the scope of this book. Instead, we provide a brief overview.

We have seen a number of circumstances in which the situation has affected the bank's prospects and operations.

» **The shareholder may be a participant in a pre-nuptial agreement that governs ownership of the stock.** A financially strong shareholder may not be quite so strong after the divorce, and established voting patterns may be disrupted.

» **A shareholder may need liquidity to finance a settlement, which could cause shares to be dumped on the market.** If the market is thin or completely illiquid, there could be a dramatic shift in the perception of the value of the stock.

» **A shareholder may be a participant to a voting agreement, while the spouse may not.** These agreements may have rights of first refusal for the participants; however, the participants may not have anticipated the need to exercise them. Do all the participants have the capability to keep shares from leaking out as a result of the divorce?

» **The combination of a divorce and a highly leveraged shareholder can be highly combustible.** It may limit the flexibility of divorcing parties in crafting a settlement, which can drag out the proceedings and possibly intensify negative feelings. This limits the shareholder's ability to promote the bank and may result in a loss of secondary financial support for the bank.

» **Distraction is a problem not just for the shareholder, but potentially for management as well.** If the shareholder is a significant owner or an executive officer, then senior officers will likely be involved and distraction can be an issue. A valuation of the shares may be performed, which requires data collection and interviews. Depositions of these officers also may be involved, which will not endear the shareholder with the deponents.

» **In the most extreme cases, a divorce can force the sale of a company.** This can be true of a community bank as well if all of the assets of the couple are in the bank. At the very least, the buyout of the "out" spouse puts leverage on the shareholder that must be serviced from somewhere. This may affect dividend policy and capital policy. Both of these affect the long-term growth potential of the bank.

SECTION SEVEN

CONCLUSION

If all the economists were laid end to end, they would not reach a conclusion.

George Bernard Shaw
Playwright

This section contains two addenda, one addressing the Capital Purchase Program, and the other Notice 2008-83 of the Internal Revenue Code, which is a tax incentive initiated in 2008 that could be beneficial for banks considering a merger or acquisition. Also, should you desire more detailed information on a specific topic, a bibliography is included. Finally, a glossary of commonly used terms is provided.

ADDENDUM

THE CAPITAL PURCHASE PROGRAM (CPP)

Note: Given that the Capital Purchase Program continues to unfold, the advantages and disadvantages of the program may evolve over time. Mercer Capital will endeavor to update our analysis as appropriate on our website (www.mercercapital.com) to reflect these developments.

OVERVIEW

In response to rapidly deteriorating conditions in U.S. financial markets, the federal government developed the Troubled Asset Relief Program ("TARP"), which became law on October 3, 2008 as part of the Emergency Economic Stabilization Act ("EESA"). Initially, the TARP was intended to allow the Treasury to purchase troubled assets from financial institutions, thereby relieving banks from illiquid assets weighing on confidence in the banking industry. The program's efforts had a slow start, however, as the Treasury faced complications in purchasing assets. In an effort among the Treasury, the Federal Reserve, and other banking regulators to address directly the growing lack of confidence in financial institutions, the Treasury announced its Capital Purchase Program ("CPP"). Through the CPP, the Treasury will use up to $250 billion of the $700 billion of TARP funds at its disposal to purchase equity stakes in banks directly in order to improve banks' capital positions and promote lending. At the time of the Treasury's announcement, the nine largest financial institutions had agreed to participate, and the Treasury committed $125 billion to these banks.

The CPP has the potential to change the banking landscape for years to come. First, the size of the program is breathtaking. According to the FDIC, the banking industry had tangible equity of approximately $870 billion at June 30, 2008.[25] The $250 billion allocated to the CPP implies that the federal government would own 22% of the industry's pro forma tangible equity. Second, the CPP could lead to a restructuring of the industry. Already, media reports have indicated that the Treasury's decision to deny National City Corporation access to the CPP impelled its sale to PNC Financial Corp., since the Treasury's denial could shake confidence in National City's viability. With few specific guidelines to aid in determining which institutions may qualify, the Treasury has assumed great power to select winners and losers in the industry. Ultimately, the CPP could accelerate the consolidation of the banking industry, as the banks denied access to the CPP (or their customers) seek the strength of other banks.

FINANCIAL ISSUES

Terms of Capital Purchases for Private Financial Institutions

Privately held community banks raised issues with the initial outline of the Treasury's program due to the implicit exclusion of private banks with the initial terms of the preferred stock purchases. Industry representatives met with Treasury officials to discuss how the program might be adapted to meet the needs of private banks, and the Treasury issued revised terms for privately held financial institutions (excluding S corporations and mutual organizations) on November 17, 2008.

Through the CPP, the Treasury will purchase senior preferred stock under standardized terms from qualified financial institutions ("QFIs"). The terms of the purchases stipulate that QFIs may issue non-voting senior preferred stock to the Treasury with a par value equal to a minimum of one percent of the bank's risk-weighted assets and up to the lesser of three percent of risk-weighted assets or $25 billion. Preferred shares issued to the Treasury must pay quarterly dividends of 5% per annum for the first five years and 9% per annum subsequently. The step-up dividend structure is designed not only to ensure that the capital injections will function as Treasury investments rather than taxpayer expenditures, but also to encourage participating banks to raise additional capital. The shares may be redeemed after three years or using the proceeds from equity offerings prior to the three year limitation. QFIs also must agree to certain restrictions on dividends and stock repurchases. Additionally, QFIs must agree to certain restrictions on executive compensation. The capital injections through the CPP will be counted as Tier 1 capital.

The terms of the preferred stock the Treasury will purchase from privately held financial institutions generally are similar to the terms for public banks, but the warrant terms have been modified. Rather than issuing warrants for shares of common stock, private banks must issue warrants for additional preferred stock with an aggregate value equal to 5% of the value of the preferred stock issued to the Treasury. The terms of the warrant preferred are the same as the terms of the "normal" preferred stock issue, except that the warrant preferred pays a dividend of 9% per year beginning on the exercise date, and the warrant preferred cannot be redeemed until all the preferred stock has been redeemed. The exercise price is negligible, and the terms state that the Treasury intends to exercise the warrants immediately, effectively increasing the preferred stock issue and increasing the dividends payable. The Treasury has indicated that certified Community Development Financial Institutions will not be required to issue warrants.

Advantages and Disadvantages of the CPP

The CPP offers terms that may be attractive to some banks, both public and private, but the Treasury's capital purchases also may pose some disadvantages to participating banks. While the following analysis of the advantages and disadvantages of the CPP is directed toward privately held banks, many of the observations are equally applicable to publicly traded banks. Given that the CPP continues to unfold, the advantages and disadvantages of the program may evolve over time.

The following table and subsequent discussion summarizes several of the key considerations for privately held banks in considering the CPP.

Factor to be Considered	Advantage/Benefit	Disadvantage/Risk
1. Dividend Rate	Lower than preferred stock issuances traded in the marketplace or issued recently	Can appear less attractive after factoring in the "cost" of the warrant and the "step-up" to 9%
2. Accessibility	Given difficult environment in which to raise capital, CPP is often more accessible than private capital	Banks may have trouble raising private capital to eventually redeem the preferred stock, resulting in the dividend stepping up to 9% and/or other restrictions
3. Ability to Use for Different Purposes	Presently, the CPP has few limitations on its use by banks, although banks are encouraged to lend	Congress could legislate how banks use the capital or regulators could exert greater pressure on banks regarding their use of the capital
4. Restrictions on Bank		CPP includes restrictions on dividends, share repurchases, and executive compensation
5. Community Reaction	Potential favorable reaction as CPP strengthens the bank's capital position and ability to lend	Potential negative reaction as the bank is seen as participating in a "bailout" and must therefore be a weaker institution

» **Dividend Rate.** One of the advantages to the CPP is the dividend rate on the preferred stock relative to preferred stock issuances traded in the marketplace. Exclusive of the warrant, the preferred stock carries a dividend of 5% for five years before it "steps-up" to 9% thereafter. Compared to yields on public preferred stock issuances, the 5% dividend is relatively low, but relative cost should not be the sole factor guiding a bank's decision to participate in the CPP. Rather, banks should consider the returns they can receive on the capital injections relative to the effective cost of the capital. When the warrants are factored in, private banks face an increased cost of capital due to the intrinsic value of the warrants at redemption as well as the 9% dividend paid on the warrants. Public banks also face a higher cost of capital due to the common stock warrants.

» **Accessibility.** In addition to offering attractive terms, the program appears to be accessible to most banks and provides a short-term solution for banks facing inhospitable markets in which to raise additional capital. Privately held banks face particularly limited options for augmenting capital, and the CPP certainly fills a void in private capital markets. Banks also must consider, however, a strategy to redeem the preferred stock in the future. Presumably, the Treasury does not intend to hold the preferred stock perpetually and has built in a dividend step-up to 9% after five years to encourage redemption of the preferred stock. Private banks may have limited options to redeem the preferred stock eventually, as raising supplemental capital may prove difficult if capital markets remain closed to instruments traditionally used by privately held banks to raise capital, such as trust preferred securities. Accordingly, private banks may be forced to de-leverage their balance sheets to redeem the preferred stock or face an increasingly high cost of capital.

» **Use of the Capital.** The terms of the CPP do not place restrictions on the use of Treasury funding, and presumably, capital injections through the CPP can be used both "offensively," by improving a bank's ability to grow, and "defensively," by affording a hedge against unanticipated deterioration in asset quality over the coming years. The CPP has the potential to encourage consolidation by providing capital to "healthy" banks, but the actual effects of the program remain to be seen. Congress already has expressed concern over banks' use of Treasury funding for acquisitions and would like to see the funding used primarily for lending. A provision in the securities purchase agreement for publicly traded banks affords the Treasury the right to amend the terms based on changes in federal statutes, and participating banks may be susceptible to restrictions on use of the capital as well as regulatory risks.

» **Restrictions.** In addition to potential regulatory risks, participating banks will face restrictions on dividends, share repurchases, and executive compensation, as stipulated in the terms of the preferred stock issuances. For private banks, share repurchase restrictions in particular could prove disadvantageous. While the CPP allows share repurchases in the normal course of business, banks with stock-based compensation arrangements or shareholders' agreements may want to consider the risks that Treasury restrictions pose. Additionally, share repurchase restrictions could reduce the liquidity of private banks' stock. Banks also have no assurance that the restrictions existing today will remain unchanged over time. A provision in the securities purchase agreement applicable to publicly traded banks explicitly states that the Treasury may "unilaterally amend" the terms to comply with changes in federal law after the funding date.

- **Community Reaction.** The publicity generated by the CPP will leave all banks, whether they apply for funding or not, subject to strong community, and customer, opinions. The Treasury is making completed transactions public, and banks that have received approval for funding seem eager to announce their participation. Banks choosing not to participate in the program could be under as much scrutiny as those on the list of participating banks. Banks that do not apply could receive questions from shareholders about their reasons for not participating if many competitors receive funding. Many of the banks that have announced they will not participate in the CPP have emphasized that they are well capitalized without the funding and simply do not need it, but, being absent from "the list" could generate concern that a bank may have been too weak to apply for the capital. Banks that apply for funding also could face adverse reactions from community members opposed to the CPP, who may consider it an unnecessary bailout plan. Additionally, customers could show concern about the financial soundness of participating banks. These concerns likely can be mitigated, however, by the extensive participation in the program among financial institutions and the support the Treasury's funding provides for a bank's capital position and growth opportunities.

VALUATION ISSUES

For privately held banks, the CPP creates a number of valuation issues.

- Initially, publicly traded banks must determine the fair value of the common stock warrants. Privately held banks also may have valuation requirements for the preferred stock warrants, although the accounting for the capital issuances by privately held banks is presently less well defined than for publicly traded banks. The accounting issues are discussed in more detail in a subsequent section of this addendum.

- The Treasury's capital purchase decisions also could affect valuations of private banks broadly through the implications of funding approval.

    - For banks participating in the program, the implications for shareholder value will vary by bank. For banks using the preferred stock primarily to buttress capital, earnings to common shareholders may suffer as value is diverted from the common shareholders to pay the preferred stock dividends. However, the increase in capital may decrease the institution's risk profile, as the likelihood of a future, unexpected capital shortfall would be mitigated. This would, other factors held constant, be a favorable development.

- For banks intending to use the preferred stock offensively to grow, the effect of the preferred stock on shareholder value will depend on the bank's ability to leverage the capital and the spread earned on the leveraged assets. One factor detracting from value, particularly over time, may be the lack of a strategy to redeem the preferred stock before the dividend steps up to 9% or the more draconian restrictions on dividends and share repurchases occur. The dividend step-up and/or the lack of capital flexibility mean that an increasingly large proportion of the bank's earnings each year would be directed over time to servicing the preferred stock.

- Banks that apply for, but do not receive, the preferred stock create interesting valuation issues as well. By denying the bank's application, the Treasury is potentially suggesting that the bank is less healthy than banks receiving the preferred stock. In this case, it may be inappropriate to apply multiples of earnings or book value derived from banks receiving the preferred stock to the stock of a subject bank that failed to gain approval for its application. By denying their application, the Treasury presumably is implying that the subject bank has a greater risk profile than the approved banks.

» When valuing privately held banks, appraisers often apply a marketability discount to consider the illiquidity of the private bank's shares. By limiting the bank's capital flexibility, such as its ability to repurchase shares, the CPP effectively is restricting the opportunities shareholders have to obtain liquidity. This could, in turn, affect marketability discounts.

The preceding list of valuation issues is not all-inclusive, given that valuation is unique to the institution. However, these identified issues provide some indication of the complex valuation issues that are likely to be created by the CPP, whether or not a bank actually participates in the program.

ACCOUNTING ISSUES

Publicly Traded Banks

For publicly traded banks, the preferred stock and common stock warrants create somewhat complicated accounting issues. In a letter dated October 24, 2008, the FASB and SEC agreed that the warrants could be included as "permanent equity," as opposed to a liability, under U.S. GAAP. Based on preliminary discussions with accounting firms, we understand that publicly traded banks first will determine the fair value of the warrants, which will be reported as a component of shareholders' equity. Then, the residual amount (the difference between the Treasury's investment and the fair value of the warrant) will be reported as preferred stock. Companies then will amortize the difference between the Treasury's investment and the recorded value of the preferred stock over the expected life of the preferred stock. To determine the fair value of the warrant, banks will use a model like the Black-Scholes option pricing model.

Consider the following example. A publicly traded bank issues $1 million of preferred stock to the Treasury, which also receives warrants to purchase $150 thousand of the bank's common stock (15% of the preferred stock issued). Using the Black-Scholes model, the bank calculates the fair value of the warrants to be $60 thousand. The bank would then record the $60 thousand warrant value as a component of shareholders' equity. The difference between the preferred stock issued ($1 million) and the warrant value ($60 thousand) is the implied fair value of the preferred stock ($940 thousand). The banks then would record preferred stock of $940 thousand and amortize the $60 thousand difference between $940 thousand and $1 million over the expected life of the preferred stock as additional dividends.

Banks should discuss the accounting ramifications of the preferred stock with their external auditors. The preceding discussion is based on preliminary discussions with accounting firms and may change as the accounting firms adopt their final positions on the accounting treatment.

Privately Held Banks

Given that the Treasury distributed the term sheet for privately held banks several days before the drafting of this addendum, we are not yet aware of any accounting guidance for the preferred stock warrants issued under the term sheet for privately held banks. One important difference between privately held banks and publicly traded banks is that, for privately held banks, the warrant is exercisable for preferred stock (rather than common stock). Further, the Treasury intends to exercise the preferred stock warrants immediately; thus, the warrants likely will not be a component of equity other than for a fleeting moment. However, the warrant preferred differs from the "normal" preferred in that the dividend is fixed at 9% (there is no 5% for five years dividend rate). Thus, banks may need to record the warrant preferred and the "normal" preferred as separate components of shareholders' equity. This may involve a determination of the fair value of the warrant preferred with the remainder of the preferred stock investment representing the implied fair value of the "normal" preferred.

The preceding discussion represents a preliminary estimate as to how accounting firms may treat the preferred stock warrants for privately held banks. Banks should consult with their accounting firms as to their research regarding the appropriate accounting.

EFFECTIVE COST OF CAPITAL FOR PRIVATE BANKS

The Treasury's capital purchases may seem to carry a relatively low cost of capital, with an initial dividend on the preferred stock of just five percent. But the value of the warrants and the dividend step-up to 9% after five years could increase the effective cost of the Treasury's capital injections substantially, depending on the length of time before the Treasury's capital purchase is redeemed. The following chart shows the effective cost of capital (i.e., the stated dividend rate on the preferred plus the "cost" of the warrants) private banks face for the preferred stock and the warrant preferred, based on the holding period of the preferred issue.

Effective Cost of Capital

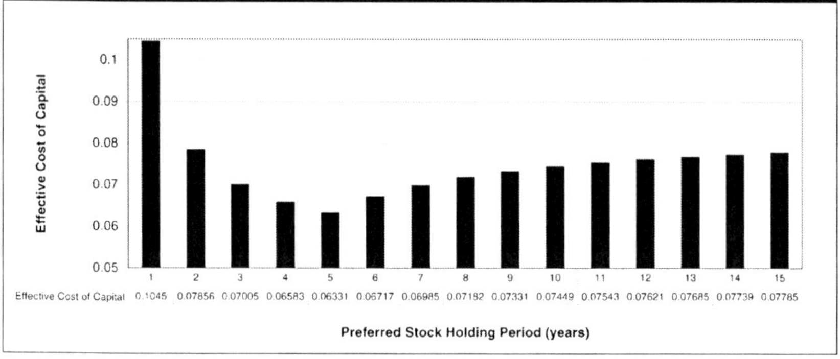

The preceding chart demonstrates an unusual pattern with the effective cost of capital dropping through year five before increasing continually thereafter. To understand this trend, consider the following:

» Since the warrants are exercisable immediately, the effective cost of capital increases to over 10% in the first year following the preferred stock issuance. Assuming a one year holding period, the bank would receive $1,000 from the Treasury today but then must repay $1,050 at the end of the one year period ($1,000 of preferred stock plus the "warrant" preferred stock equal to 5% of $1,000) plus dividends on $1,050 (5% on $1,000 of the preferred stock and 9% on the warrants of $50). Therefore, the cost of the preferred stock is actually over 10.45% [(Dividends paid out of $54.50 + Warrants redeemed of $50) / Preferred Stock of $1,000] if the preferred stock is redeemed after only one year.

» The exercise price of the warrants is negligible, but the par value of the warrant preferred must be 5% of the aggregate value of the preferred stock issued to the Treasury, so the "value" of the warrant preferred essentially is fixed. Thus, as the holding period of the preferred stock is extended, the cost of the warrant preferred value is spread out over a longer time period.[26]

- » After five years, the dividend on the "normal" preferred stock also increases to 9%, and the effective cost of capital increases continually thereafter. As the holding period increases, the bank pays the 9% dividend rate for proportionately more years, thereby leading to the rising cost of capital after the fifth year.

- » The effective cost of capital always will remain higher than the initial 5% dividend paid on the preferred stock issue as the warrant preferred carries a 9% dividend and cannot be redeemed until the preferred stock has been redeemed in full.

While the Treasury presumably structured the preferred stock to encourage banks to accelerate the redemption of the preferred stock, the structure of the preferred stock warrant for privately held banks actually creates the opposite incentive. A bank seeking to minimize the effective cost of capital will postpone the redemption of the preferred stock until the fifth year, following which the dividend step-up to 9% outweighs the beneficial impact of postponing redemption of the warrant preferred stock.

The Treasury announced that certified Community Development Financial Institutions ("CDFIs") will not be required to issue warrants. For such banks, the effective cost of capital simply will be the effective dividend rate on the preferred stock issue, which was discussed previously and is shown in the following chart.

Effective Dividend Rate on Preferred Stock

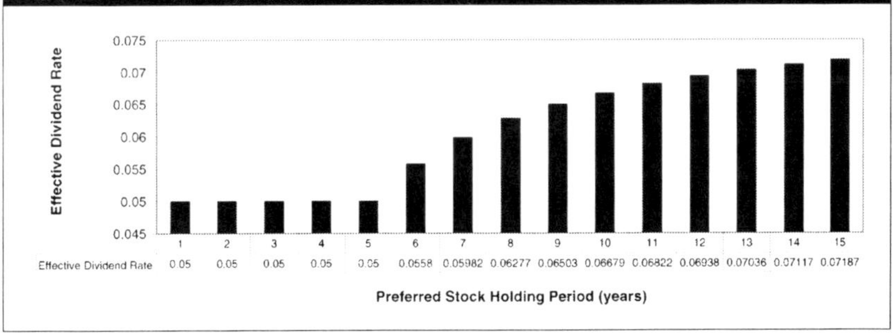

EFFECTIVE COST OF CAPITAL FOR PUBLIC BANKS

For public banks, the analysis of the effective cost of capital is more complicated. In addition to the effect of the dividend step-up feature, the effective cost of capital is susceptible to changes in the price of the bank's common stock that underlies the common stock warrants. The value of the common stock is, in turn, a function of market valuation multiples and the bank's financial performance. We have developed a model to determine the effective cost of the Treasury's capital injections, including the common stock warrants, based on varying assumptions regarding market price/tangible book value multiples and the growth in tangible book value over the holding period.[27]

The extent to which each of these assumptions affects the cost of the Treasury's capital purchases can be analyzed best by considering each assumption in isolation. The uncertainty of the warrant value is perhaps the most significant factor in determining the effective cost of capital under the CPP. The warrant value, which will equal the set number of warrants issued multiplied by the change in the stock price over the holding period, is primarily a function of the stock pricing multiples at the initial purchase and the exercise date and growth in tangible book value over the holding period. The more price/tangible book value multiples improve over the holding period, the more valuable the warrants and the greater the effective cost of capital.

Holding the growth rate in tangible book value constant at 8% and assuming a five-year holding period, the following chart presents the range of the implied cost of capital based on varying price/tangible book value multiples. As shown in the chart, the effective cost of capital will be 6.24% if the pricing multiples do not change from the issue date to the exercise date (which we assume is the date of the preferred stock redemption). If the pricing multiples improve, however, the cost of capital will increase. For instance, if the price/tangible book value multiple rises from 100% at issuance to 150% at exercise, the effective cost of capital increases from 6.24% to 8.07%.

Even if pricing multiples remain flat or continue to decline over the holding period, growth in the bank's tangible book value will increase the value of the warrants, driving up the effective cost of capital. The preceding analysis assumed an annual growth rate in tangible book value of 8%. If, however, tangible book value grows more quickly, the implied cost of capital could increase. Assuming a five-year holding period, the following chart shows the range of the cost of capital based on varying pricing multiples if the annual growth rate in tangible book value were 10%. Continuing the preceding example (a price/tangible book value multiple of 100% at issuance and 150% at exercise), the effective cost of capital increases to 8.58% assuming 10% growth in tangible book value, versus 8.07% assuming 8% growth in tangible book value.[28]

Implied Cost of Capital - Five Year Holding Period

Initial Price/TBV	Price/TBV at Exercise Date						
	100.0%	**125.0%**	**150.0%**	**175.0%**	**200.0%**	**225.0%**	**250.0%**
75.0%	7.48%	8.66%	9.78%	10.86%	11.90%	12.90%	13.87%
100.0%	6.24%	7.17%	8.07%	8.94%	9.78%	10.60%	11.39%
125.0%	5.47%	6.24%	6.99%	7.72%	8.42%	9.11%	9.78%
150.0%	5.00%	5.60%	6.24%	6.87%	7.48%	8.07%	8.66%
175.0%	5.00%	5.13%	5.69%	6.24%	6.78%	7.31%	7.82%
200.0%	5.00%	5.00%	5.28%	5.76%	6.24%	6.71%	7.17%

Alternatively, slower growth would imply a lower cost of capital, holding all else equal. The following chart presents the range of the cost of capital given 5% annual growth in tangible book value over a five-year holding period.

Implied Cost of Capital - 5% Growth in Tangible Book Value

Initial Price/TBV	Price/TBV at Exercise Date						
	100.0%	**125.0%**	**150.0%**	**175.0%**	**200.0%**	**225.0%**	**250.0%**
75.0%	6.84%	7.89%	8.90%	9.87%	10.81%	11.72%	12.59%
100.0%	5.74%	6.57%	7.37%	8.14%	8.90%	9.63%	10.35%
125.0%	5.06%	5.74%	6.40%	7.05%	7.68%	8.30%	8.90%
150.0%	5.00%	5.17%	5.74%	6.29%	6.84%	7.37%	7.89%
175.0%	5.00%	5.00%	5.25%	5.74%	6.22%	6.68%	7.14%
200.0%	5.00%	5.00%	5.00%	5.31%	5.74%	6.16%	6.57%

Assuming a five-year holding period and constant pricing multiples over the holding period, a 5% tangible book value growth rate implies a 5.74% cost of capital, while 8% growth implies a 6.24% cost of capital, and 10% growth implies a 6.61% cost of capital.

Implied Cost of Capital - 10% Growth in Tangible Book Value

		Price/TBV at Exercise Date						
		100.0%	**125.0%**	**150.0%**	**175.0%**	**200.0%**	**225.0%**	**250.0%**
Initial Price/TBV	**75.0%**	7.94%	9.20%	10.41%	11.57%	12.68%	13.74%	14.76%
	100.0%	6.61%	7.61%	8.58%	9.51%	10.41%	11.28%	12.13%
	125.0%	5.77%	6.61%	7.41%	8.20%	8.96%	9.69%	10.41%
	150.0%	5.20%	5.91%	6.61%	7.28%	7.94%	8.58%	9.20%
	175.0%	5.00%	5.40%	6.01%	6.61%	7.18%	7.75%	8.31%
	200.0%	5.00%	5.02%	5.56%	6.09%	6.61%	7.11%	7.61%

The dividend step-up feature of the preferred stock certainly will increase the cost of capital substantially if the preferred stock is not redeemed by 2014. Additionally, the value of the warrants will build over a longer holding period, assuming the bank's tangible book value is growing each year. The following table shows the range of the implied cost of capital based on varying price/tangible book value multiples, given a six-year holding period and an 8% growth rate in tangible book value.

Implied Cost of Capital - Six-Year Holding Period

		Price/TBV at Exercise Date						
		100.0%	**125.0%**	**150.0%**	**175.0%**	**200.0%**	**225.0%**	**250.0%**
Initial Price/TBV	**75.0%**	7.84%	8.83%	9.77%	10.68%	11.54%	12.37%	13.18%
	100.0%	6.80%	7.58%	8.34%	9.07%	9.77%	10.45%	11.11%
	125.0%	6.15%	6.80%	7.43%	8.04%	8.63%	9.21%	9.77%
	150.0%	5.70%	6.26%	6.80%	7.33%	7.84%	8.34%	8.83%
	175.0%	5.58%	5.86%	6.34%	6.80%	7.25%	7.69%	8.13%
	200.0%	5.58%	5.58%	5.98%	6.39%	6.80%	7.19%	7.58%

As shown in the following table, which again assumes an 8% growth rate in tangible book value, the effective cost of capital can be quite high if the holding period is extended to the ten-year maximum holding period of the warrants.

Implied Cost of Capital - Ten-Year Holding Period

Initial Price/TBV	*Price/TBV at Exercise Date* 100.0%	125.0%	150.0%	175.0%	200.0%	225.0%	250.0%
75.0%	8.50%	9.12%	9.71%	10.27%	10.81%	11.32%	11.80%
100.0%	7.84%	8.34%	8.81%	9.27%	9.71%	10.13%	10.54%
125.0%	7.42%	7.84%	8.24%	8.62%	9.00%	9.36%	9.71%
150.0%	7.13%	7.49%	7.84%	8.17%	8.50%	8.81%	9.12%
175.0%	6.92%	7.24%	7.54%	7.84%	8.12%	8.41%	8.68%
200.0%	6.76%	7.04%	7.31%	7.58%	7.84%	8.09%	8.34%

Extending the holding period, while holding the pricing multiples constant over the holding period and assuming an 8% growth rate in tangible book value increases the effective cost of capital from 6.24% over a five-year holding period to 6.80% over a six-year holding period and 7.84% over a ten-year holding period.

The following chart indicates the effective cost of capital over different holding periods, assuming:[29]

» No change in the price/tangible book value multiple between issuance and exercise.

» An increase in the price/tangible book value multiple from 100% at issuance to 150% at exercise.

» An increase in the price/tangible book value multiple from 100% at issuance to 200% at exercise.

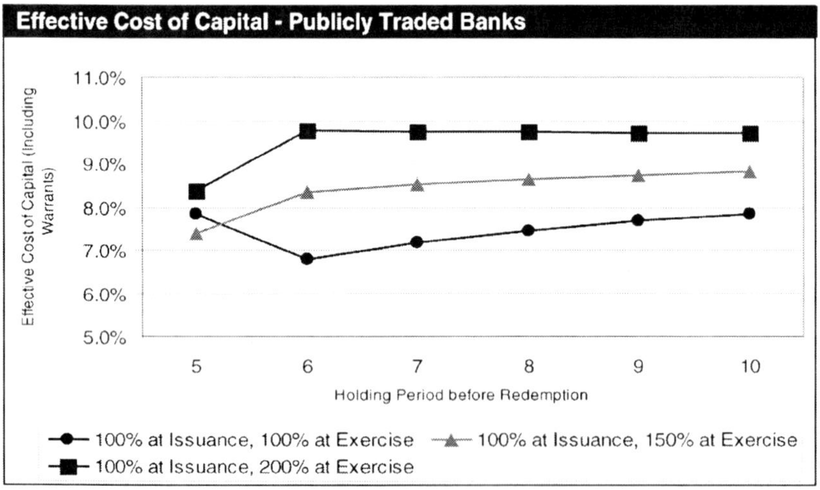

A bank, therefore, should develop expectations about market pricing, growth prospects, and the length of time before the preferred stock will be redeemed, before deciding to participate in the CPP, as such assumptions could affect the true cost of the Treasury's capital purchases significantly.

ADDENDUM

IRS PROVIDES NEW TAX INCENTIVE FOR BANKS

On October 1, 2008, the IRS issued Notice 2008-83, which changes the way banks can recognize losses on loans or bad debts in a change of control transaction.

Up until Notice 2008-83, Section 382 of the Internal Revenue Code provided limits on the utilization of net operating loss carry forwards against future taxable income of any new loss corporation following the ownership change. Section 382 provides that, after an ownership change, the amount of a loss corporation's taxable income for any post-change year available for offset by pre-change NOLs shall not exceed the Section 382 limitation for that year. The Section 382 limitation equals the fair market value of the corporation's stock as of the change date, multiplied by the long term tax exempt rate (currently about 4.65%). The Section 382 limitation represents the hypothetical return on a loss corporation's value had it not undergone an ownership change. By limiting the absorption of NOLs to the hypothetical return of a loss corporation, Congress attempted to eliminate tax bias for or against the sale of loss corporations based on their NOLs.[30] Accordingly, the key here is relating post-change taxable income to losses that are recognized post-change, but may have been implicitly unrecognized pre-change. In other words, if the target bank has significant bad loans on its books, loans that were generated pre-change, the prior system of applying Section 382 would have limited the losses available to be recognized for deductions by the acquiring bank based on the application of the formula in Section 382. The regulatory action which changes that is reproduced below.

Notice 2008-83 is separate and distinct from the Emergency Economic Stabilization Act of 2008 ("EESA"), but was clearly coordinated through the Treasury, and comes at a helpful time for the nation's troubled financial system. In addition to the bad mortgage loans that were the initial and precipitating consideration for the credit crunch, the investment assets such as mortgage-backed securities and collateralized debt obligations would appear to be included as bad debt instruments.

APPLICATION OF SECTION 382(H) TO BANKS

Notice 2008-83
Section 1. Overview

The Internal Revenue Service and Treasury Department are studying the proper treatment under Section 382(h) of the Internal Revenue Code (Code) of certain items of deduction or loss allowed after an ownership change to a corporation that is a bank (as defined in Section 581) both immediately before and after the change date (as defined in Section 382(j)). As described below under the heading Reliance on Notice, such banks may rely upon this guidance unless and until there is additional guidance.

Section 2. Treatment of Deductions Under Section 382(h)

For purposes of Section 382(h), any deduction properly allowed after an ownership change (as defined in Section 382(g)) to a bank with respect to losses on loans or bad debts (including any deduction for a reasonable addition to a reserve for bad debts) shall not be treated as a built-in loss or a deduction that is attributable to periods before the change date.

Section 3. Reliance on Notice

Corporations described in Section 1 of this notice may rely on the treatment set forth in this notice, unless and until there is additional guidance.[31]

IMPLICATIONS FOR THE FINANCIAL INSTITUTIONS MARKETPLACE

Moreover, the revised regulation applies to more than what we think of as a traditional bank. As defined in Section 581 of the Internal Revenue Code, the term "bank" means a bank or trust company incorporated and doing business under the laws of the United States (including laws relating to the District of Columbia) or of any State, a substantial part of the business of which consists of receiving deposits and making loans and discounts, or of exercising fiduciary powers similar to those permitted to national banks under authority of the Comptroller of the Currency, and which is subject by law to supervision and examination by State, Territorial, or Federal authority having supervision over banking institutions. The term also means a domestic building and loan association.[32]

At this writing, the scope of the bad loans and debts held on the books of the nation's financial institutions is substantially unknown, but the size of the $700 billion EESA program implies a clear and present danger. For those banks and bank holding companies that have been relatively unscathed by the financial crisis, this additional incentive to acquire troubled banks with significant bad loans or debts on the books is compelling.

As reported in the *New York Times*, Wells Fargo's rejuvenated bid for Wachovia on Thursday, October 2, 2008, at a price greatly exceeding that of rival Citigroup, was clearly based on the "advantage of a lucrative tax loophole tied to deferred losses," and could be structured to avoid any direct government support.[33] While the deal was initially suspended by the court, the validity of the tax incentive was not at issue, and was obviously substantial. Citigroup had agreed to a $2.2 billion deal when Wells Fargo came in at $15.4 billion.

Additional consolidation in the U.S. banking system appears assured, given the severity of the financial crisis. For banks with reasonable profitability and growth prospects, this appears to be a propitious time to acquire market share and utilize the tax incentive of being able to deduct the expected losses from bad loans and debt obligations against future earnings.

BIBLIOGRAPHY

GOVERNMENT RESOURCES

The Federal Deposit Insurance Corporation

www.fdic.gov

The Federal Deposit Insurance Corporation maintains the stability of and public confidence in the nation's financial system by insuring deposits made at banks and monitoring banks' risk. The FDIC Quarterly Banking Profile provides a comprehensive summary of financial results for all FDIC-insured institutions and presents significant trends in the banking industry. The FDIC also provides deposit market share data for all FDIC-insured banks by geographic area.

The Federal Financial Institutions Examination Council

www.ffiec.gov

The Federal Financial Institutions Examination Council is an interagency body for the various regulatory agencies overseeing financial institutions. The FFIEC prescribes uniform principles, standards, and report forms for regulated financial institutions and provides regulatory filings of quarterly financial data (such as Call Reports and Y-9 filings) for FDIC-insured financial institutions.

The Community Development Financial Institutions Fund

www.cdfifund.gov

The Community Development Financial Institutions Fund provides credit, capital, and financial services to underserved populations and communities in the United States through direct investment in community development with the CDFI program and through financial incentives (including tax credits and Bank Enterprise Awards) and support to banks that invest in underserved communities.

The Federal Reserve System

www.federalreserve.gov

The Federal Reserve System is the United States' central bank, and in addition to conducting monetary policy and setting interest rate levels, the Fed regulates national and member financial institutions, holds bank reserves, and provides additional liquidity to banks. The Federal Reserve website also provides statistical releases including historical interest rate releases.

The Office of Federal Housing Enterprise Oversight

www.ofheo.gov

The Office of Federal Housing Enterprise Oversight (now known as the Federal Housing Finance Agency) regulates and supervises the two government-sponsored housing enterprises, Fannie Mae (the Federal National Mortgage Association) and Freddie Mac (the Federal Home Loan Mortgage Corporation). The agency also provides annual reports to Congress regarding Fannie Mae's and Freddie Mac's financial performance and compliance with regulatory standards.

The U.S. Small Business Administration

www.sba.gov

The U.S. Small Business Administration provides assistance to small businesses through loans, loan guarantees, contract opportunities, and support. The agency also provides research and statistics and a comprehensive list of small business laws and regulations to assist small businesses.

The U.S. Securities and Exchange Commission

www.sec.gov

The U.S. Securities and Exchange Commission is the primary overseer of the U.S. securities markets. The SEC regulates the securities markets and enforces compliance with securities laws. The SEC also maintains registration statements, financial performance reports, and other regulatory filings for all reporting companies, which are available for public access.

The U.S. Department of Labor

www.dol.gov

The Department of Labor fosters and promotes the welfare of the working, retirees, and unemployed in the United States. The DOL is the primary regulator of employee benefit plans. Their website has a number of resources on retirement plans and related topics.

The Internal Revenue Service

www.irs.gov

The Internal Revenue Service is a bureau of the Department of Treasury and oversees tax administration in the United States.

NEWS AND INFORMATION

Bloomberg

www.bloomberg.com

Bloomberg is a reliable, comprehensive information source for business and financial professionals. Bloomberg Online provides global news articles, current and historical market data including stock, bond, commodity and fund prices and indices, as well as investment tools.

The Wall Street Journal Online

www.wsj.com

The Wall Street Journal Online provides the Web edition of its daily newspaper, as well as market data and tools including stock prices and indices, currency prices, interest rate information, and economic reports. Much of the news provided by the *Wall Street Journal* is available only to subscribers, but the market data and tools are publicly available.

American Banker

www.americanbanker.com

American Banker is a print newspaper and an online subscription service with articles and information about the banking and financial services industries. *American Banker* also provides subscribers with bank data, including benchmark profiles and rankings of banks.

Bankstocks.com

www.bankstocks.com

Bankstocks.com provides free research and commentary about the financial services industry. The website provides links to various news headlines and offers commentary on market conditions as well as on specific companies.

Bank Director

www.bankdirector.com

Bank Director is a print and web-based magazine that serves as an information source for senior officers and directors in the financial services industry. *Bank Director* offers articles on mergers and acquisitions, retail strategies, and other relevant topics in banking. The website also provides a supplemental resources center that is published quarterly.

SNL Financial

www.snl.com

SNL Financial is a research firm that provides subscribers with information and financial analysis for the banking, specialized financial services, and insurance industries, in addition to real estate, energy, and media/communications industries. SNL provides market and industry data as well as company data including corporate structure and officer information, deposit information, merger and acquisition information, financial performance data, and peer comparisons, for both public and private companies.

Standard and Poor's

www.standardandpoors.com

Standard and Poor's provides credit ratings, indices, equity research, risk analysis tools, data services including company and market data, and investment advisory services. The S&P website offers public access to credit ratings and various indices, including the S&P/Case-Schiller Home Price Indices, which measure the change in residential housing prices in metropolitan regional indices, composite indices, and a national index.

ASSOCIATIONS AND ORGANIZATIONS

Mercer Capital

www.mercercapital.com

Mercer Capital is an independent financial advisory firm specializing in consulting, business valuation, and investment banking services, including financial reporting and tax valuation, M&A advisory, fairness and solvency opinions, ESOP and ERISA valuation services, and litigation support.

The American Bankers Association

www.aba.com

The American Bankers Association is the largest banking trade association in the country. The ABA represents banks, bank holding companies, savings banks, and trust companies through legislative and regulatory activities, legal action, communication, and research.

Bankers Online

www.bankersonline.com

This website has a number of different links and provides articles and additional information on the banking industry. Links to a number of financial services websites can be found on the site, as well as links to the national and state bankers associations.

The ESOP Association

www.esopassociation.org

The Employee Stock Ownership Plan Association is a non-profit membership association that promotes and enhances laws that govern ESOPs while promoting employee ownership in companies. The ESOP Association also publishes the ESOP Report, which provides regulatory and case law updates and other relevant information for ESOPs.

The American Society of Appraisers – BV Accreditation

www.bvappraisers.org

The American Society of Appraisers provides professional accreditation for specialized appraisers including business valuation appraisers, and offers training courses, seminars, and conferences for business appraisers. The ASA also has developed a *Code of Ethics and Business Valuation Standards* and was involved in developing the Appraisal Foundation's *Uniform Standards of Professional Appraisal Practice*.

The Financial Accounting Standards Board

www.fasb.org

The Financial Accounting Standards Board establishes and improves the authoritative standards of financial accounting and reporting in the U.S. in order to maintain the usefulness of financial reporting. The FASB website provides updates on FASB activities and additions to the accounting literature, as well as the full text of Statements of Financial Accounting Standards and other FASB pronouncements.

Hovde Organization

www.hovde.com

Hovde Organization is an investment banking, asset management, and private equity firm focused exclusively on the financial services sector. In addition, Hovde publishes financial services industry updates, M&A transaction summaries, and a monthly overview of the financial services industry.

Insights for Bank Directors

www.stlouisfed.org

Insights for Bank Directors, provided by the Kansas and St. Louis Federal Reserve Banks, is a basic course for banking directors that covers evaluation of financial performance, portfolio risk, loan review, regulatory issues, market and liquidity risk, and the allowance for loan losses.

The Board of Directors Network

www.boarddirectorsnetwork.org

The Board of Directors Network is an organization that advocates for more women both in executive leadership and on corporate boards to improve corporate governance through diversity. The Board of Directors Network produces an annual study relating the composition of corporate boards of directors as well as a shareholders guide regarding proxy votes and board diversity.

The Corporate Executive Board

www.executiveboard.com

The Corporate Executive Board provides research and analysis related to strategy, operations, and management to its membership of large, prestigious organizations. The Corporate Executive Board uses its members as case study examples for researching solutions to the challenges faced by companies today.

The Corporate Directors Forum

www.directorsforum.com

The Corporate Directors Forum is a non-profit organization that promotes improved corporate governance through education and peer networking. In addition to providing networking opportunities to its members, the Corporate Directors Forum also provides informational documents regarding corporate governance for public access.

The Environmental Bankers Association

www.envirobank.org

The Environmental Bankers Association is a non-profit trade organization representing the financial services industry that promotes environmental risk management and sustainable development lending through formal meetings, news, articles, and research documents available to members.

The National Association of Corporate Directors

www.nacdonline.org

The National Association of Corporate Directors is a non-profit membership organization providing services related to corporate governance. The NACD provides a monthly publication with corporate governance information, research and benchmarking data, online forums, and other corporate governance resources.

The Conference Board

www.conference-board.org

The Conference Board is a business membership and research organization, providing members with research covering sustainability, economics, ethics, governance, marketing, risk management, and other relevant business topics. The Conference Board provides economic forecasts as well as the Consumer Confidence Index and the Leading Economic Indicators.

The American Association of Bank Directors

www.aabd.org

The American Association of Bank Directors is a banking trade association that serves individual directors of financial institutions. The AABD website provides a number of resources for bank directors, including information on a number of seminars, books, and studies pertaining to the role of financial institution directors.

BOOK REFERENCES

Books Written by Mercer Capital

The following books are available at www.mercercapital.com.

Business Valuation: An Integrated Theory, Second Edition,
(John Wiley & Sons, Inc., 2008)

Business Valuation: An Integrated Theory, Second Edition enhances understanding and application of fundamental valuation concepts. Thoroughly revised and expanded, the *Second Edition* demystifies modern valuation theory, bringing together various valuation concepts to reveal a comprehensive picture of business valuation.

Buy-Sell Agreements: Ticking Time Bombs or Reasonable Resolutions?
(Peabody Publishing, LP, 2007)

In *Buy-Sell Agreements: Ticking Time Bombs or Reasonable Resolutions?*, the professionals of Mercer Capital speak from their own experiences valuing hundreds of business interests for purposes of buy-sell agreements. You will gain insight into the potential folly of fixed-price or formula pricing, common misunderstandings that can end up as big money issues, and the pitfalls of buy-sell templates. Single and multiple appraiser process agreements are explored in depth. In addition, the six defining valuation elements of process buy-sell agreements are presented in depth for the first time.

Valuing Shareholder Cash Flows: Quantifying Marketability Discounts
(Peabody Publishing, LP, 2005)

The Quantitative Marketability Discount Method presents a practical model to assist business appraisers in developing, quantifying and defending marketability discounts under the income approach. The model allows you to quickly and easily quantify marketability discounts in the appraisal of minority business interests.

Valuing Financial Institutions
(Business One Irwin, 1992)

Valuing Financial Institutions is an indispensable reference for anyone involved with the valuation of banks, bank holding companies, thrift institutions, thrift holding companies, or other financial institutions. It was the first and only comprehensive, how-to treatise on the valuation of financial institutions written in the mainstream of business valuation theory and practice.

ARTICLE AND NEWSLETTER REFERENCES

Mercer Capital's Article Library

www.mercercapital.com

Mercer Capital's article library provides a compilation of numerous financial institutions articles written by professionals at Mercer Capital.

Mercer Capital's Bank Watch

www.mercercapital.com

Sign up at Mercer Capital's website for monthly or quarterly newsletters, including Mercer Capital's monthly *Bank Watch*. *Bank Watch* is published by Mercer Capital's Financial Institutions Group, and profiles completed transactions, follows key indices of top financial institutions, and provides insight into financial institution valuation issues.

GLOSSARY

In the following section, valuation terms are quoted from the American Society of Appraisers, ASA Business Valuation Standards© (Revision published July 2008). Banking-related terms are quoted from the book Valuing Financial Institutions, by Z. Christopher Mercer, ASA, CFA, (Homewood, IL, Business One Irwin, 1992).

Appraisal – The act or process of determining the value of a business, business ownership interest, security, or intangible asset. The objective of an appraisal is to express an unambiguous opinion as to the value of a business, business ownership interest, security, or intangible asset which opinion is supported by all procedures that the appraiser deems to be relevant to the valuation.

Asset (Asset-Based) Approach – A general way of determining a value indication of a business, business ownership interest, security, or intangible asset using one or more methods based on the value of the assets net of liabilities.

Asset Sensitivity – A bank may be described as asset sensitive when the earnings impact of a change in the interest rate environment is greater for its assets than its liabilities. For example, a bank with an asset sensitive balance sheet position typically will benefit from rising rates, as the asset base reprices more quickly than the liabilities. Conversely, an asset sensitive balance sheet generally would be adversely impacted in a falling interest rate environment.

Basic Operating Income – A measure of profitability. Basic operating income is described as fully taxable equivalent pre-tax income before the loan loss provision and gains or losses on securities transactions. That is, it equals net interest income, plus non-interest income, minus non-interest expenses.

BOLI – An acronym for "bank-owned life insurance."

Book Value – The difference between a bank's assets and liabilities (also known as shareholders' equity).

Brokered Deposits – Bank deposits solicited by a third-party broker. Brokered deposits are typically, but not always, deposits for some amount slightly below

$100,000 in order for all interest as well as principal to be covered by deposit insurance. Brokers typically are paid a fee by the depository bank.

Business Valuation – The act or process of determining the value of a business or ownership interest therein.

Calculations – The objective of a calculation is to provide an approximate indication of value based on the performance of limited procedures agreed upon by the appraiser and the client.

Controlling Interest Basis – Refers to the value of the enterprise as a whole.

Control Premium – The difference between the value of a subject interest that exercises control over the company and the value of that same interest lacking control (but enjoying marketability). In practice, the control premium is generally expressed as a percentage of the marketable minority value.

Core Deposits – Core deposits are typically a bank's least interest-sensitive deposit liabilities. Core deposits generally include non-interest bearing demand accounts, interest-bearing transaction accounts, savings accounts, and money market deposit accounts ("MMDAs"). Some definitions of core deposits also include time deposits less than $100,000.

Discounted Future Benefits Method – A method within the income approach that develops a valuation indication based on a projection of a future stream of benefits, the present value of which represents the indication of value of the subject bank.

Efficiency Ratio – A measure of a bank's level of overhead expense relative to the revenue base. The efficiency ratio is calculated as operating expenses divided by adjusted gross income (net interest income plus non-interest income). Unlike most other profitability measures, a lower efficiency ratio is preferable to a higher one.

Fair Value (Accounting) – The standard of value in a number of valuation issues related to financial statement reporting. It is defined in paragraph 5 of FAS 157 as: "The price that would be received to sell an asset or paid to transfer a liability in an orderly transaction between market participants at the measurement date."

Fair Value (Statutory) – A standard of value applicable to situations involving appraisal rights of dissenting minority shareholders arising from certain corporate actions such as mergers, reorganizations, or recapitalizations. Fair value in the statutory context is recognized as the applicable standard of value in most states. Fair value is defined generally by judicial interpretation of the relevant statute.

Fair Market Value – The price, expressed in terms of cash equivalents, at which property would change hands between a hypothetical, willing and able buyer and a hypothetical willing and able seller, acting at arms' length in an open and unrestricted market, when neither is under compulsion to buy or sell and when both have reasonable knowledge of the relevant facts.

FHLB Advances – Loans granted to member financial institutions by Federal Home Loan Banks. FHLB advances are structured to meet a wide variety of borrower needs. Common structures include bullet advances, putable advances, and principal reducing credit advances.

Financial Controlling Interest Basis – Refers to the value of the enterprise, excluding any revenue and expense synergies that may accrue to a strategic buyer. This level of value is viewed from the perspective of a financial buyer, who may expect to benefit from improving the enterprise's cash flow and its capital structure but not through any operating synergies that may be available to a strategic buyer.

Guideline Public Company Method – A method within the market approach that utilizes the pricing of guideline public companies, adjusted for any fundamental differences between the subject company and guideline public companies, to develop an indication of value of the subject bank.

Income Approach – A general way of determining a value indication of a business, business ownership interest, security, or intangible asset by using one or more methods that count anticipated economic benefits into a present single amount.[41]

Loan Loss Reserve – The valuation reserve against total loans; it represents an amount believed to be adequate to cover probable incurred losses in the portfolio. The loan loss reserve is increased by loan loss provisions and recoveries of prior loan charge-offs and reduced by loan charge-offs.

Market Approach – A general way of determining a value indication of a business, business ownership interest, security, or intangible asset by using one or more methods that compare the subject to similar businesses, business ownership interests, securities or intangible assets that have been sold.

Marketability Discount – An amount or percentage deducted from the value of an ownership interest to reflect the relative absence of marketability.

Marketable Minority Interest Basis – Refers to the value of a minority interest, lacking control, but enjoying the benefit of liquidity as if it were freely tradable in an active market.

Merger and Acquisition Method – A method within the market approach that develops an indication of value for a subject company based on change of control transactions.

Minority Interest Discount – The difference between the value of a subject interest that exercises control over the company and the value of that same interest lacking control (but enjoying marketability). In practice, the minority interest discount is expressed as a percentage of the controlling interest value.

Net Asset Value Method – A method within the asset-based approach that develops a valuation indication in the context of a going concern by adjusting the reported book values of a subject company's assets to their market values and subtracting its liabilities (adjusted to market value, if appropriate). The indicated value should not be interpreted as an estimate of liquidation value.

Net Charge-Offs – Total loans and leases charged off the balance sheet, less recoveries on previously charged-off credits.

Net Interest Margin – Net interest income as a percentage of average earning assets. It also can be defined as the yield on average earning assets less the cost of funding those earning assets.

Net Spread – The yield on average earning assets, less the cost of interest-bearing liabilities. The net spread measures the absolute difference in rates earned and rates paid. The net spread is lower than the net interest margin because it does not include the effect of non-interest bearing funding sources.

Non-Accrual Loans – Typically, a loan is placed on non-accrual status due to sufficient deterioration of the borrowers' financial condition to the point that collection of principal and interest is jeopardized. When a loan is placed on non-accrual status, previously accrued and unpaid interest income is written off and interest accrual generally ceases. Payments received are applied to the loan's principal.

Nonmarketable Minority Interest Basis – Refers to the value of a minority interest, lacking both control and market liquidity.

Non-Performing Assets (or Loans) – Non-performing assets are defined as loans past due 90 or more days, non-accrual loans, OREO, and restructured loans. A non-performing asset represents a potentially greater risk to the bank than a performing asset, but not all non-performing assets result in losses to the bank.

OREO – An acronym for "other real estate owned," or real estate other than bank premises owned or controlled by a bank. This account includes foreclosed property and is carried at the lower of cost or market value.

Return on Assets – A measurement of how profitably assets are used by a bank. Return on assets ("ROA") equals net income divided by assets.

Return on Equity – Measures the interplay between the profitability of the bank's asset base (as measured by ROA) and its leverage (represented by the equity multiplier, or assets divided by equity). Return on equity ("ROE") equals net income divided by shareholders' equity.

Strategic Controlling Interest Basis – Refers to the value of the enterprise as a whole, incorporating the strategic intent that may motivate particular buyers and the expected synergies that may result from an acquisition.

Tangible Equity – The amount of stockholders' equity after deduction of intangible assets (generally other than mortgage servicing rights).

Transactions Method – A method within the market approach that develops an indication of value based upon consideration of actual transactions in the stock of a subject bank.

Trust Preferred Securities – Securities possessing characteristics of both equity and debt instruments. A bank issues trust preferred securities by first creating a trust (a special purpose entity). The trust then issues trust preferred securities, which pay distributions at fixed or floating rates, to investors. The trust then uses the cash raised to invest in subordinated debentures issued by the bank holding company. Because the interest paid on the debentures is tax-deductible, the bank may realize tax benefits from the issuance of trust preferred securities. The trust preferred proceeds generally are includable in a bank's regulatory capital.

Wholesale Borrowings – Borrowing consisting of non-core liabilities including brokered CDs, FHLB advances, and Fed Funds purchased. Wholesale funding typically is used to fund the asset base in the absence of sufficient deposit growth or to increase flexibility in asset/liability management.

ENDNOTES

In addition to the specific references listed, a significant portion of this book relies upon a number of books, articles, and other materials prepared by Mercer Capital professionals. The most notable of these would be the book *Valuing Financial Institutions,* by Z. Christopher Mercer, ASA, CFA, (Homewood, IL, Business One Irwin, 1992).

1 American Society of Appraisers, *ASA Business Valuation Standards©* (Revision published July 2008), "Glossary."

2 American Society of Appraisers, *ASA Business Valuation Standards©* (Revision published July 2008), "BVS I, General Requirements for Developing a Business Valuation©."

3 Ibid.

4 Ibid.

5 American Society of Appraisers, *ASA Business Valuation Standards©* (Revision published July 2008), "Glossary."

6 Ibid.

7 For example, debt with below-market internal rates or very high risk contingency payments could not be converted into cash at their nominal amounts.

8 IRS Revenue Ruling 59-60

9 Mercer, Z. Christopher and Harms, Travis W., *Business Valuation: An Integrated Theory, Second Edition* (John Wiley & Sons, Inc., 2008).

10 American Society of Appraisers, *ASA Business Valuation Standards©* (Revision published July 2008), "Glossary."

11 Ibid.

12 Ibid.

13 Ibid.

14 American Society of Appraisers, *ASA Business Valuation Standards©* (Revision published July 2008), Statement SBVS-1, Guideline Public Company Method.

15 American Society of Appraisers, *ASA Business Valuation Standards©* (Revision published July 2008), Statement SBVS-2, Guideline Transactions Method.

16 It is important to note that the spread between the option price and the option stock's fair market value constitutes an adjustment item for alternative minimum tax purposes.

17 The limitations on the inclusion of preferred stock and trust preferred securities in regulatory capital are based on the regulatory capital guidelines specified in Title 12, Part 225 – Bank Holding Companies and Change in Bank Control (Regulation Y), Appendix A, B, D, and E to Part 225 – Capital Adequacy Guidelines for Bank Holding Companies.

18 The information in this chapter serves as a brief overview of buy-sell agreements. If you are seriously considering creating a buy-sell agreement or have questions about a buy-sell agreement already in place, we suggest that you look to a book on the subject written by Chris Mercer, CEO of Mercer Capital. *Buy-Sell Agreements: Ticking Time Bombs or Reasonable Resolutions?* which covers valuation topics related to buy-sell agreements in much greater detail.

19 "Empirical Evidence Confirming the Importance of a Transaction Advisor," by Jay Wilson, Jr., August 21, 2007. Available at www.mercercapital.com.

20 www.fdic.gov.

21 This example is constructed such that the bank retains $450 in both the C corporation and S corporation scenarios. In the C corporation scenario, the bank has after-tax income of $650 but pays dividends of

$200. In the S corporation alternative, the bank has pre-tax income of $1,000 and makes distributions of $550 (inclusive of the tax and economic distributions).

22 SFAS 157, Paragraph 5.

23 AICPA Center for Audit Quality, Measurements of Fair Value in Illiquid (or Less Liquid) Markets, October 3, 2007.

24 Per SFAS 107.

25 Per the June 30, 2008 Quarterly Banking Profile published by the FDIC.

26 In fact, the effective cost of the preferred stock would continue to decline as the holding period increases, because of the bank's ability to defer redemption of the warrant preferred stock. This effect is obscured in the chart because the dividend rate steps up to 9% after the fifth year.

27 Our model estimates the effective cost of capital using the value of the warrants as of the date of the preferred stock redemption. However, the warrants could be exercised several years after the preferred stock is redeemed, which could modify the effective cost of capital.

28 By restricting dividend payments and stock repurchases, the Treasury is not only reducing the risk that the bank may not be able to redeem the preferred stock. It is also potentially increasing the value of the warrants, as these capital restrictions may serve to increase the growth in tangible book value.

29 All three scenarios assume 8% growth in tangible book value.

30 Internal Revenue Service Technical Advice Memorandum, No. 200217009, December 4, 2001.

31 Application of Section 382(h) to Banks, Notice 2008-83, www.irs.gov.

32 Internal Revenue Code, Section 581 Definition of a Bank.

33 "Citigroup Says Judge Suspends Wachovia Deal," *The New York Times,* October 5, 2008.

ABOUT MERCER CAPITAL

For those readers not familiar with Mercer Capital, please forgive us for a gentle "plug" about our firm and our services. Mercer Capital is a leading employee-owned independent financial advisory firm offering a broad range of consulting and investment banking services, including financial reporting and tax valuation, M&A advisory services, fairness and solvency opinions, ESOP and ERISA valuation services, and litigation support. For over 25 years, Mercer Capital has provided financial advisory services to a broad range of clients including public and private companies in hundreds of industries.

Focus On Financial Institutions

Mercer Capital has a long history of providing valuation services to financial institutions. Mercer Capital's Financial Institutions Group provides a wide range of valuation, investment banking, and industry expertise to assist banks, thrifts, mortgage banks, money managers, broker/dealers, insurance companies, and REITs.

Our banking clients are diverse in terms of both location and size, ranging from new de-novo banks to multi-billion dollar (assets) bank holding companies. We have worked for numerous governmental agencies, including the Internal Revenue Service, the Federal Deposit Insurance Corporation, the Small Business Administration, the U.S. Attorney General's Office, and the Attorney General of the State of Tennessee.

Our work has been reviewed and accepted by the major agencies of the federal government, including the Securities and Exchange Commission, the FDIC, the Federal Reserve, the Office of Thrift Supervision, and the Office of the Comptroller of Currency. Our work also has been reviewed by the largest firms in the nation in connection with transactions involving their clients.

Valuation Services

Mercer Capital is routinely retained by financial institutions across the country to provide valuation services, some of which are summarized below.

» **Mergers, Acquisitions, and Corporate Reorganizations** - We are regularly engaged in transactions involving the purchase and sale of financial institutions. We have acted as a financial advisor by providing the fairness opinion and/or assisting in the negotiations. We also have extensive experience in valuations for stock sales and repurchases and transactions, which trigger dissenting shareholder rights.

» **Financial Statement Reporting** - We have provided numerous valuations of employee stock options and restricted stock. In addition, we provide purchase price allocation services for core deposit valuations (FAS 141), mark-to-market accounting for assets and liabilities, goodwill impairment (FAS 142), and contracts such as non-compete and employment agreements.

» **Litigation Support and Expert Testimony** - We have been retained as financial and/or valuation experts in many litigated situations, including: business damages; lost profits; buy-sell agreements; securities fraud analyses; family law and marital dissolution; blockage analyses; bankruptcy and corporate reorganization issues; ESOP matters and other ERISA-related disputes; and a review of expert reports for potential rebuttal testimony or cross examination purposes. Our professionals have testified in numerous state and federal courts.

» **Employee Benefit Plans** - We provide valuations for employee stock ownership plans, employer stock held in 401(k) plans, and stock options.

» **Tax Compliance** - We have prepared numerous appraisals for estate tax purposes, family limited partnerships, gifting programs, and charitable gifts.

Transaction Advisory Services

If a decision to undertake a transaction has been made, Mercer Capital can assist in the process through the following:

» **Advise, Structure, and Negotiate Mergers, Acquisitions and Other Transactions** - We are an active advisor to community banks for purposes of selling to and acquiring other institutions. Our role ranges from initiating and structuring transactions on behalf of clients to providing fairness opinions and other support advisory services for transactions that largely were negotiated by the institutions' management.

» **Issue Fairness Opinions** - Fairness opinions are an integral part of most transactions for sellers and, if the transaction is large enough, for buyers. Generally, legal counsel to institutions with more than a few shareholders will suggest that sellers obtain a fairness opinion to provide comfort to the board of directors that the consideration received in a transaction is fair to shareholders from a financial point of view.

» **Provide Strategic Alternative Analysis to Enhance Shareholder Value** - We are engaged regularly by financial institutions to provide shareholder assessments regarding strategies to enhance shareholder value. Such actions include a "sell-now vs. sell-later" evaluation, as well as capital management activities such as increasing dividend payout ratios, share repurchase programs, and cash acquisitions.

» **Financial Advisor to Independent Board Committees** - We have served as financial advisor to a number of boards for purposes of providing ongoing advisory services as well as providing advice from a financial perspective in special circumstances, such as transactions, that require an independent board committee.

» **Branch Acquisition Analyses** - Community banks have, and will have, an increasing opportunity to acquire branches which are being divested by regional and super-regional institutions that are paring their branch networks or complying with anti-trust orders. Mercer Capital can assist in the bidding process by providing valuation, bidding, and negotiating support.

» **Provide Research** - We maintain extensive databases on public market and acquisition pricing of banks, thrifts, insurance companies, REITs, broker-dealers, and money managers. In addition, our research capabilities allow us to produce detailed peer comparisons for most institutions.

For more information, visit our website at www.mercercapital.com.

THE MERCER CAPITAL LIBRARY

Access information on the following products at www.mercercapital.com

BOOKS

BUY-SELL AGREEMENTS: TICKING TIME BOMBS OR REASONABLE RESOLUTIONS?

Written for business owners, attorneys, CPAs, business appraisers, and other professional advisors to business, this book provides a road map for you (or your clients) to develop or improve your buy-sell agreement. Learn from our 25 years of experience working with well-constructed and not-so-well constructed buy-sell agreements (in almost every case no one realized there were problems until a trigger event occurred!).

BUSINESS VALUATION: AN INTEGRATED THEORY, SECOND EDITION

Whether you are an accountant, auditor, financial planner, or attorney, *Business Valuation: An Integrated Theory, Second Edition* enables you to understand and correctly apply fundamental valuation concepts. Thoroughly revised and expanded, the Second Edition demystifies modern valuation theory, bringing together various valuation concepts to reveal a comprehensive picture of business valuation.

REVENUE RULING 59-60 AT 50

This book offers a guided tour through the Ruling and pulls back the curtain a bit, granting a non-technical view of how appraisers attempt to translate the guidance found in Revenue Ruling 59-60 into actual valuation engagements.

NEWSLETTERS

Bank Watch

Brought to you by the Financial Institutions Group of Mercer Capital, *Bank Watch* is a complimentary monthly publication that profiles completed transactions, follows key financial institutions indices, and provides insight into financial institution valuation issues. To subscribe, visit www.mercercapital.com.

Value Added™

Published 4 times per year, *Value Added*™ provides a broad overview of our latest thinking, containing articles relating to all aspects of business valuation, including controversy services, financial statement reporting, gift & estate tax, shareholder disputes, ESOPs, and transaction-related topics. To subscribe, visit www.mercercapital.com.

Value Matters™

Value Matters™ is published approximately 10 - 12 times per year and is designed to bring targeted, timely, and topical business valuation-related information to our readers who consist primarily of attorneys, CPAs, and other advisors to business. To subscribe, visit www.mercercapital.com.

Value Focus Industry Outlooks

Having built a substantial client base in various industries, we have formalized our research efforts to provide a regular, detailed overview of pertinent issues and relevant current events. Mercer Capital's latest publication, *Value Focus*, offers a quarterly perspective on valuation issues pertinent to various industry groups and sectors. Each issue of Value Focus includes a segment focus, market overview, mergers and acquisitions review, and more. To subscribe, visit www.mercercapital.com.

ORDER ADDITIONAL COPIES OF

THE BANK DIRECTOR'S VALUATION HANDBOOK

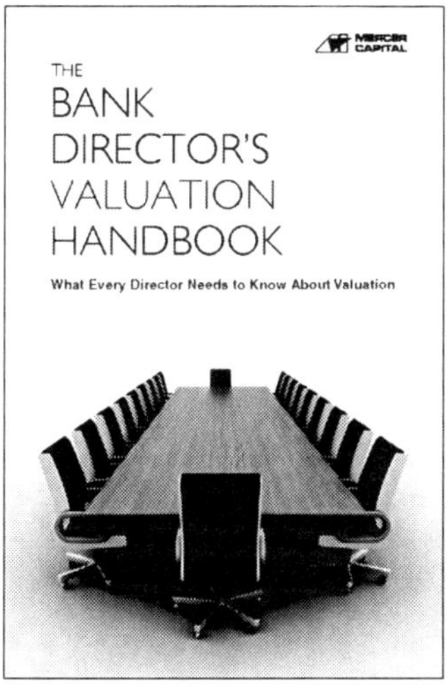

Order a copy for each member of your board and management team.

- » 1-5 copies at $55.00 per book*
- » 6 or more copies at $29.00 per book*

** Shipping and sales tax not included*

To order, call Barbara Walters Price at 901.685.2120 or via email at priceb@mercercapital.com.

Mercer Capital
5860 Ridgeway Center Parkway, Suite 400
Memphis, TN 38120
901.685.2120 (P) :: 901.685.2199 (F)

Printed in the United States
139830LV00001BA/1/P